W9-BNH-244

POWER WRITING,
POWER SPEAKING

POWER WRITING, POWER SPEAKING

200 WAYS TO MAKE YOUR WORDS COUNT

COMPILED AND EDITED

by N. H., S. K., *and* P. S. Mager

WILLIAM MORROW AND COMPANY, INC.
NEW YORK   1978

Grateful acknowledgment is made to the following for permission to reprint quotations: Peter De Vries, Dean Rusk, Fletcher Knebel for material from June 1975, May 1961, and October 1961 *Reader's Digest* respectively, reprinted with permission from *Reader's Digest*. Knebel selection also reprinted courtesy The Register and Tribune Syndicate, Inc. "Four" by Eloise Gibbs reprinted from *The Saturday Evening Post* copyright © 1955 The Curtis Publishing Company. Selection from "In Praise of Stark Lucidity" by Bruce Price reprinted by permission of *Princeton Alumni Weekly*. Quotation from *Fishbait* by Miller and Leighton © 1977 by William Moseley Miller and Frances Spatz Leighton, published by Prentice-Hall, Inc., Englewood Cliffs, N.J. Ogden Nash poem reprinted by permission of Little, Brown and Company. Excerpts from *The Greatest Laughs of All Time* by Gerald Lieberman, copyright © 1961 by Gerald F. Lieberman; used by permission of Doubleday & Company, Inc. "Rocket" from *Kaddish and Other Poems* by Allen Ginsberg copyright © 1961 by Allen Ginsberg; reprinted by permission of City Lights Books. Quotation from "Old Em's Kentucky Home" by Damon Runyon reprinted by permission of American Play Co. as agents for Damon Runyon Estate. Quotations from Joey Adams reprinted by permission of the author. Selection from Daffynitions from *The Wall Street Journal* reprinted by permission of Cartoon Features Syndicate.

Library of Congress Cataloging in Publication Data

Mager, Nathan H. (date)
    Power writing, power speaking.

    Includes index.
    1. Figures of speech.   2. English language—Rhetoric.
3. Persuasion (Rhetoric)   I. Mager, Sylvia K. (date)
II. Mager, P. S., joint author.   III. Title.
PE1445.A2M25   808'.042   78-15230
ISBN 0-688-03295-8

BOOK DESIGN   CARL WEISS

Printed in the United States of America.

First Edition

1   2   3   4   5   6   7   8   9   10

To THE MULTITUDE OF GREAT MINDS *who have con-tributed to this compilation—those who have explored the labyrinths of rhetoric and those who have lent their wisdom to illustrate these rhetorical concepts—the editors gratefully dedicate this text, with sincere thanks for the pleasures in discovering them.*

PREFACE

THIS WORK WAS BEGUN IN AN ATTEMPT TO COLLECT SOME OF the unusual ways people could put words together effectively. Our first step was to collect the well-turned phrases that have been remembered and quoted; then by a process of induction, we planned to identify the techniques and describe them.

We asked ourselves: What is it that makes a phrase, a sentence, a paragraph so memorable and powerful that it becomes part of a nation's verbal syndrome, to be recalled and repeated, even to become a force in people's lives?

> "Four score and seven years ago . . ."
> ". . . We have nothing to fear but fear itself."
> ". . . footsteps on the sands of time."
> "Neither a borrower nor a lender be . . ."

The sentiment, of course, the occasion—yes, who said it! But most phrases we repeat express thoughts that were not unique to the time or place or person whose words we repeat. They are part of the human heritage, largely because of the way they were said.

Midway in our assembling it became apparent that someone had done all this before—that there already were names for all the identifiable devices. In fact, each device had many names—identified by rhetoricians—some of which were common knowledge almost to the time of our grandparents.

As we compiled and collated, we found that rhetoric had a long and fascinating history, much too intricate to be detailed here, but sufficiently relevant to be part of the explanation of the devices that still could be—and are, albeit subconsciously—used by the modern writer or speaker.

The result is this volume, which is, we hope, a guide to techniques that are widely used but seldom identified, techniques that were long taught, but are now sublimated and dependent on innate talent in writing.

Even just naming a technique, we felt, would be helpful in bringing it to greater use. Our "how-to" approach has been more extensive. From the thousand or more rhetorical devices identified and named in thousands of years, we have selected two hundred of the most useful, and we have explained them in three ways:

1. By describing the device itself.
2. By listing the various names that have been applied to the device, which are themselves descriptive.
3. By providing examples sufficient to show the application of the techniques in a twentieth-century world and to help you apply them.

Undoubtedly there will be scholars who feel that much of both the history and the discussion is superficial. But nonscholars—the vast majority of ordinary speakers and writers —will undoubtedly find much that is new, interesting, refreshing, and useful. If you wish to make your own words more persuasive, appealing, and vivid, you will find it easy to adapt the techniques described here for your own uses. By studying the quotations, you can draw parallel phrases or create similarly startling twists of words.

For whatever the reader may find to be irrelevant or pretentious or unduly "lifted" from the words of wise people in many generations, we apologize. Where we could recall or locate the sources, we were pleased to acknowledge them. Where we could not, we express our regrets. We must add, however, that discovering and compiling the wisdom of rhetoricians and pundits has been one of the most joyful adventures of many years of research. It is a special kind of pleasure that comes from "discovering" something that has been around us all the time.

CONTENTS

CHAPTER

I

THE POWER OF THE WORD

ABOUT 427 B.C. A GREEK NAMED GORGIAS ARRIVED IN Athens with the discovery of a series of techniques that could convince almost anyone of anything. Many called it magic. The techniques were not entirely new; primitive tribes had had advance men for their armies who used some of these devices to convince invading forces to turn around and go home.

Some poets, philosophers, literary critics, grammarians (such as Protagoras), and some orators had noted and used the devices as early as the ninth century B.C. (Homer for example). Hesiod in the eighth century, and Pindar (called the first European literary critic) in the sixth century B.C., used some of them. Many rhetorical devices were used in the Bible. Some orators—Empodocles, Tisias, and Corax—wrote early textbooks. But Gorgias put it all together for wider consumption and became the target of critics and the defender of the system.

Some Greeks were very much upset by the new science. Plato deplored it vigorously. After all, if persuasion became a special skill of the few, what would happen to truth and justice? But Aristotle set about putting it all in order in what became known as Aristotelian rhetoric. Cicero and many others improved on the science for two thousand years. Until a hundred years ago, rhetoric was the most important part of a college education.

* * *

The science of rhetoric had very dramatic beginnings. One of the first to use it, even before Gorgias, was Archilochus. Archilochus was born on the island of Paros in the seventh century B.C. of humble parents—his mother was a slave. He was betrothed to Neobule, the daughter of Lycambes, a local aristocrat.

Suddenly Lycambes "broke the great oath made by salt and table" and refused to sanction the marriage—perhaps because Archilochus made public the facts of his socially low parentage. In a terrible rage that followed, Archilochus composed iambics against his not-to-be in-laws, and sang them at the festival of Demeter. What followed is described by Hipponax, a sixth century B.C. poet who was banished from Ephesus for writing insulting verse: Archilochus "so cursed them with bitterness and biting labels," that Lycambes and Neobule were shamed, and "they knit their necks in halters and so hanged themselves."

Hipponax, a small misshapen man, sensitive about his appearance, also insulted the aristocracy. A later historian, Theocritus, noted: "Here lies the bard Hipponax. If you are a rascal, go not nigh this tomb, but if you are a man of good stock, sit you down and welcome."

After he was killed in battle Archilochus became the center of a cult on Paros. (His killer was banished for having slain a great poet.) The epitaph notes: "Cerberus, whose bark strikes terror into the dead, there comes a terrible shade before whom even thou must tremble. Archilochus is dead. Beware the acrid iambic wrath engendered by his bitter mouth."

Until that time, the bards had sung mostly about the gods. Archilochus garnered his reputation as a troubadour in the Aegean by publicizing his personal troubles and triumphs, establishing a reputation as a satiric—and venomous—poet, a man in a perpetual rage about something. For a millennium he ranked in fame with Sophocles, Pindar—almost next to

Homer. Some thought his words had the power of a curse, so often did they bring death or destruction to his victims.

During many generations afterward, the poet's satire was viewed as a sort of witch's curse—even more, a call for punishment from the gods—and a thing to be dreaded. Poets were said to have occult powers. In fact, the Twelve Tables, the first written version of Roman Law (fifth century B.C.), invokes the death penalty for only two crimes: for using magic to entice a neighbor's crops into one's own field; and for chanting an evil charm against someone.

RHETORIC AT WAR

The phenomenon of the magic of words was not limited to the West. It grew wherever man could hurl an invective.

Arabic poetry is divided into two types—encomium and satire—both considered magical in the pre-Islamic world. The poet was the oracle of the nomadic tribes, considered to have supernatural wisdom. He was a warrior, and his secret weapon was the high hija—his words. Satire could be fatal: The curses of the disheveled, sandal-shod poet, leading warriors in battle, was the psychological weapon of the time. Shouting imprecations was a black magic in which both the nation's warriors and their foe believed. Individuals also met in the field of honor, like knights in the age of chivalry, raising as their weapons only ridicule, insult, epithet, obscenity, humor—usually in extemporaneous verse.

Honor was vulnerable and more precious than life. Some poets carried their trade to civilian life, reciting improvised panegyrics to those who paid well, and ridiculing and abusing those too stingy to contribute. The trade was not limited to men. Muhammad, a peaceful man, is said to have ordered the execution of two women satirists. On another occasion he noted that the satires of three poets "caused more damage . . . than a whole flight of arrows."

References to the power of words are also found in the

Bible: Dancing women who in song ascribed the slaying of thousands to Saul, but tens of thousands to David, so upset Saul that he sought David's death. The songs of Deborah (Judges)—some never published—are credited with stirring up the Jewish tribes against the women of Jenin for centuries after.

In Ireland in the ninth century the poet was a warrior of no mean power. Here is an extract from an old document:

> "And thou, O Carpre, son of Eain," saith [King] Leigh to his poet, "what power can you wield in battle?"
> "Not hard to say," quoth Carpre, "I will make a glam dicind on them. And I will satirize them and sam them, so that through the spell of my art they will not resist warriors."

The island had a long prehistoric tradition of satiric poetry. Some rulers found poets so threatening that they were banished. In A.D. 515, a thousand poets were ordered by King Ald to leave the country because their numbers and "exactions" were intolerable. A compromise pact, ratified by the saints, reduced the number of poets and put limitations on their venom.

POET AS PUNDIT

Almost everywhere, the poet, with his superior command of language in his little-educated society, was medicine man, prophet, preacher, historian, lawyer.

Not all poets spent their prowess in a courtly manner. In the East, Jarwal ebn Aus (the Dwarf) was a wandering minstrel in prose, moving from tribe to tribe reciting panegyrics. His principal reward came from those he did not mention—a sort of protection racket. Eventually he landed in jail in the "interest of public safety." A similar technique was made notorious by gossip sheets in the nineteenth century in Europe and America.

* * *

In his day, the troubadour was economist, journalist, historian, and publicist. His words established praise or blame. For the uneducated population, the poet and the druid were virtually identical. Their malefic doses of satire—voiced by men or women—were actionable by civil suit, often under the same regulations that made criminal assault, theft of cattle, or sexual attack on a man's wife. By law, the rank of the injured was the gauge of the damage. The treatment of women by satirists was particularly censorious. A woman who was satirized by her husband "until she is laughed at" in public, however, might leave him and regain her dowry. Satire was permitted, even encouraged, for a public cause—such as the collection of taxes.

A fragment remains of one controversy involving Master Morprelate:

> I am a rimer of the Irish race.
> And have already rimde thee staring mad;
> But if thou cease not thy bold jests to spread
> I'll never leave til I have rimde thee dead.

In many other parts of the world, too, the rhetoric of ridicule was an effective sanction. Many primitive societies considered mockery as severe a punishment as death—and in some later societies, notably among the Japanese, the Pueblo Indians, and the Eskimos, suicide was, and to an extent still is, the ultimate choice after derision or disgrace.

PUNISHMENT BY RHETORIC

Among the Tlingit Indians of southeastern Alaska, crimes for shameful acts (we might call them victimless crimes) were punishable by public ridicule with songs composed by professional writers and effigies posted in the public square. Suicide was not an uncommon result of such ridicule.

The sanction of verbal ridicule was similarly utilized among many primitive tribes of the Americas and Africa, where loss of respect in a community left few alternatives. Exile to the hostile environment was fatal, and suicide was often the only answer.

One study of the Ashanti of West Africa describes the horror of being laughed at. If one broke wind while food was being served, "the bowl of food would be placed upon the offender's head, so the rest of the gathering could use him as a table." If the man was among friends and was well liked, the others would hide their laughter at his ridiculous position. But if the man was not respected and the party laughed openly at him, he would probably hang himself.

The tradition of the malevolent rhetorician has lived through the generations among wandering minstrels and troubadours, court jesters, and critics until our own times. For actors, political figures, and others in the public eye, ridicule can mean the end of a career. For all of us, words said publicly are often enough to bring the torments of shame, guilt, and the loss of self-esteem.

Rhetoricians have also served a variety of other functions— praising, entertaining, and rousing people to a feeling of community. In primitive cultures the storyteller was often not only a diverting performer, but also the teacher of morality and history. Many of the minstrels, troubadours, and court jesters also stressed jolly entertainment and enlightenment. Some rhetoricians have reached high position through flattery, others have stirred hearts with revolt—traditions still alive today with poet laureates and political pundits.

What happened then, to the magical science of rhetoric?

It went underground. A few universities still teach it, but for the most part, people who write or speak effectively usually pick up these techniques of rhetoric subconsciously. This is, of course, not the best thing that could have happened. Almost everyone could probably write or speak more movingly, more convincingly, more vividly, by consciously applying a little of this old magic.

CHAPTER

II

ALL ABOUT RHETORIC

WHEN IT WAS DEVELOPED, RHETORIC HAD AN IMPACT ON society as great as that of dynamite or the atom bomb. It revolutionized society and placed skills in the hands of certain educated citizens, giving them powers of life and death over their fellow citizens.

HUMBLE ORIGINS

Rhetoric began to be widely understood in the fifth century B.C., as we have noted, when Gorgias of Leontini, Sicily, noticed that people reacted more readily to some forms of expression than to others. Gorgias attributed the great power of rhetoric to two elements—poetry and magic.

In his drama *Helen*, Gorgias's heroine announces the news: "The divine charms working through words can bring both pleasure and pain." Gorgias soon went on to list expressions that he thought were so powerful that they could be used for "magic and witchcraft." He saw poetry itself as a sort of magic—an offshoot of music, which he also thought was magical. Essentially, he saw rhetoric as a means of persuasion that could convince people of anything, regardless of the truth. When tragedy developed as a literary form, it became evident that rhetoric could produce "shuddering fright and weeping pity" and even "sorrowful longing."

Early masters of rhetoric claimed a special, virtually magical power to evoke fear and other emotions in their listeners and, later, to achieve more subtle responses. Gorgias found that speech could stop fear and banish sorrow, inspire joy, develop pity, produce fright or confidence. Those discoveries became the basis for a new technology, as a device for power —much like the machine gun or the computer in modern times—as orators, playwrights, poets, and others vied to create the most moving expressions for their audiences. Thrasymacher became famous for the ability to produce sorrow, anger, or tranquillity in an audience. Sophocles, in his last play, noted that words could move people—producing pleasure, displeasure, or pity.

Of course many of the elements of rhetoric were used by the Greeks even before Gorgias. Antithesis, for example, is found in much early poetry. But it was Gorgias who stimulated the use of rhetoric and who organized it into a science of writing and speaking. He adapted the techniques of poetry, which he saw as a sort of proto-rhetoric, to prose use. His devices included punning, wordplay, rhyme, rhythm, and such balanced sentences as this from his play *Epitaphios:*

> arrogant for what brings profit, passionate for what is proper, insolent, moderate, terrible in things terrible.

And in his play *Helen,* he uses, "destiny's intention, or the god's decision, or necessity's compulsion." The public accepted Gorgias's rhetoric not only as magic, but as a breakthrough in verbal science—and so it was for his time.

Wisely, Gorgias noted that speech—like magic or drugs— could be used for good or bad, to poison or cure, for right or wrong.

A TECHNIQUE FOR DECEIT

Rhetoric was so potent, it seemed, that immediately a great concern arose as to its use for bad and for good—that is, the ethical use of this new "weapon." Ever since, rhetoricians have argued the moral obligation of the writer or speaker to use his skills for good rather than for self-interest or evil.

Plato, who was a conservative in the modern sense, saw in rhetoric a technique for deceit. (He even deplored the inaccuracy of poetry.) He was terrified by the evil influence it could have in daily life, especially in politics, such as in persuading judges, counselors, and the legislature without regard to truth and justice. One of Plato's contemporaries compared rhetoric to magic, calling it a science of illusion, the equivalent of a magician's ability to call up phantoms and to make people believe in things that do not exist. He cites the example of Thucydides, when the Spartan king asked him who was the better fighter, he or Pericles:

> "When I have knocked Pericles down in a fight," said Thucydides, "he says he didn't fall, and wins the fight by persuading the people."

THE PRACTICAL ART

Aristotle, on the other hand, saw rhetoric as a practical art, even a science of persuasion. He listed and classified the elements of rhetoric—the disposition of the audience, the emotional factors, the types of reasoning and logic, and the various figures of speech involved. In this way, he made rhetoric a respectable science. Where Gorgias offered a quick way to a practical result, Aristotle offered rules. Where it was before gimmickery for persuasion, Aristotle made it a science of analyzing the possibilities in each situation, a process of reasoning.

Rhetoric became a parallel to dialectic, the science of weighing arguments to arrive at the truth. Thus Aristotle removed the label of magic from persuasive speech, and placed the whole subject in the basket of logic. The aim of rhetoric became clarity; metaphors and other devices were used to make ideas more understandable, not as obfuscation.

Typically, Aristotle also neatly listed all the methods of presenting an argument, including ten ways of misleading people into accepting a point of view:

1. Conclude an argument as if at the end of a reasoning process, without bothering to take your audience through the processes.
2. Play on illogical, fortuitous similarity of words. (A saucepan must be noble because the great god Pan was noble.)
3. Make a statement about the whole that is true only of individual parts, or vice versa.
4. Use indignant language.
5. Use a single, unrepresentative example.
6. Take the accidental as essential.
7. Argue from consequence. If something turned out right from the principle, the principle was right.
8. Argue *post hoc, ergo propter hoc*. If something happened after an act, it was because of the act.
9. Ignore crucial circumstances.
10. Make out, from fraudulently confusing the general and the particular, that the improbable is probable, and vice versa.

In his work Aristotle succeeds in giving philosophical values to the theory of the art of speaking. He subordinates the techniques of ethics, politics, and psychology. He views rhetoric as a practical psychology for everyone whose business it is to persuade—writers, lawyers, legislators—all of us. In today's literary marketplace, his subject might well be: "How to frame a speech."

For classicists, rhetoric is the *sine qua non* of instruction in writing. Aristotle's *Treatise on Rhetoric* is called "a magazine of intellectual riches" by Lane Cooper in *The Rhetoric of Aristotle*:

"His principles are the result of extensive original induction. He sought them, if ever man did seek them, in the living pattern of the human heart. All the recesses and windings of that hidden region he has explored, all its caprices and affections, whatever tends to excite, to ruffle, and amuse, to gratify, or to offend it, have been carefully examined. The reason of these phenomena is demonstrated, the method of creating them is explained.

"The whole is a textbook of human feeling, a storehouse of taste; an example of condensed and accurate, but uniformly clear and candid reasoning."

CICERO THE ORGANIZER

Cicero, two and a half centuries after Aristotle, was the great "modern" organizer of rhetoric. He fused the theories of oratory and poetry in a manual on persuasion, and his theories and terminology have been long lasting. Cicero's classical rhetoric is based on the work of Demosthenes and his contemporaries into a framework for effective oratory. It entered the English language during the lifetime of The Venerable Bede (673–735) in five stages. Until the end of the Middle Ages, rhetoric was (with the possible exception of grammar) the most important field of study in language.

Cicero's rhetoric was divided into five procedures of communication, which he called Invention (discovering the facts or arguments), Arrangement (placing them in order), Style (putting them in proper language), Memory (getting a mental grasp of the material), and Delivery (control of voice and gestures). Cicero left no text but his ideas were perpetuated in a later work of unknown authorship: *Ad C. Herennium Libre Quattuor De Arte Rhetorica*. In this, each of the categories was given equal weight.

During the Renaissance (and, in fact, until the end of the nineteenth century), rhetoric was taught principally as an aid to organization and delivery of an oration, but most of those who studied the subject understood that rhetoric was involved in all forms of effective communication as well. The educated man of the Middle Ages was required to master grammar, logic, and rhetoric for a bachelor's degree, plus arithmetic, music, geometry, and astronomy for a master's degree. These were the seven basic arts.

INTO THE CURRICULUM

In the seventeenth century the emphasis changed. "Stylistic" rhetoric was committed to the doctrine that style was the most important of the five elements. This was developed in the Latin text *Institutio Oratoria* by Marcus Fabius Quintilianus (A.D. 35–95), known as Quintilian.

The "formulary pattern" was a third fashion in rhetoric. It developed the study by model compositions for guiding students in the art of communications. The great work in this tradition was "The Art of Rhetoric" by Thomas Wilson (1553), which devotes sixty-eight percent of its text to invention, twenty-one percent to style. It ran through many editions and was the handbook of William Shakespeare.

The Ramistic theory of communications was based on the work of the philosopher Pierre de la Ramée (1515–1572), known as Petrus Ramus in his early years. A thesis on Ramus's three laws was required for graduation from Harvard and most other institutions of higher learning. This pattern assigned invention and arrangement to dialectic, and style and delivery to rhetoric.

Latter-day rhetoric was commonly divided into three parts —organization, invention, and expression—a reduction from the seven parts into which it had been classified in some earlier periods: exordium (introduction), narration (how the matter came up for discussion), exposition (explaining the meaning of the issues), proposition (what is to be proved), confirmation (the arguments), refraction (denying the opposition), and peroration (conclusion). The contemporary approach defines these parts simply as a beginning, a middle, and an end.

Two English writers added definitive catalogs of rhetorical devices during the seventeenth century. These are now noted for their whimsy as much as for their analyses. The elements that we note as figures of speech—metaphor, simile, hyperbole, personification—were known then (as indeed they are today) as tropes.

Tropes or figures were part of every man's literary learning of the time. George Puttenham (1529-1590)—some say it was his brother Richard—wrote an updated version of rhetoric called *The Arte of English Poesie* in 1589. The treatise on versification gave new descriptive titles to the Greek and Roman concepts, titles which seem quaint to us today. Henry Peacham (1576-1643) compiled the *Garden of Eloquence* and primers on art (*The Gentleman's Exercise,* 1607) and conduct (*The Compleat Gentleman,* 1622) that discussed these techniques. Peacham was a schoolmaster, a traveling tutor, and a self-appointed authority on cosmography, drawing, sculpture, music, poetry, heraldry—and, or course, rhetoric.

RHETORIC TODAY

Each of us can recall from history a time when someone has spoken in sentences that have moved the world, even changed the course of history. It is not for every man to have the opportunity—or the talent—to present a "cross of gold" speech or to let go a quip to be heard around the world.

Then why did we dismiss this ancient art? It is not that we do not appreciate the poignancy of the "old" rhetorical way of saying things. Perhaps we associate rhetorical devices with their archaic uses and think that they dilute sincerity, confuse communication, or clutter our utterances with superfluous language. And devices and ornaments of every kind are frowned upon in this era of relaxed freedom. But devices of rhetoric need not be flowery or supercilious. With proper understanding of what they are and why they work, they can and do add color, and help us express many thoughts more precisely.

Like Molière's "bourgeois gentilhomme," who was surprised to learn that he was speaking in prose all his life, most of us may not give a second thought to rhetorical devices in daily use. But we do use the many techniques first named and cataloged by the Greeks, widely developed by the Romans, and made into something of a religion during the century between 1650 and 1750.

The word "rhetoric" itself has diffused much of its original meaning. Aristotle discussed it as the art of argument—a sort of poetry of persuasion. A later concept concentrated on "the embellishment of thought by verbal ornamentation." As a result, rhetoric developed a bad name. It became synonymous with pretentious, ornate expression. Although Webster's Third devotes twenty-eight lines to various definitions, many people today understand it as merely the use of words rather than deeds: "He is all rhetoric." Academicians prefer to define it as "the art of effective oral and written communication"—skill in the use of expressive or moving ·speech—in short, eloquence.

As in Aristotle's time there is an antirhetoric school today. It holds that rhetoric is "just words, without meaning," "inflated language," "verbosity, bombast." "That passage, sir, is not empty rhetoric," Virginia Woolf noted. Philip Rahv speaks of "The enemy of rhetoric and every kind of artifice and virtuosity." Stanley Baldwin called it "the harlot of the arts."

At least one writer of keen perception, William Safire, who was a key speech writer for President Nixon and a firsthand observer of the assassination of rhetoric, sees us in the age of "antipolingo"—an era of misty, anodyne vagueness, where speech says as little as possible. By not using figures or other rhetorical devices, authors and speakers are not likely to awaken the listener and rouse him to action, he says.

Basic to all theories of rhetoric is the "figure." A figure is simply an unusual way of using words, a device or pattern of language through which the presentation of a message is changed or enhanced. Many figures have been classified by succeeding rhetorical authorities, and their Greek names have often bowed to more modern terminology.

Most widely recognized today are the figures of speech—metaphor, simile, onomatopoeia, alliteration—all together, sometimes called trope. In the figures of speech, words are deliberately given meanings other than their ordinary literal meanings so that ideas appear fresh and vivid. Other figures have been termed "schemes," because they are made up of a pattern of words usually involving the structure of a sentence. Through the generations, thousands of devices have been identified.

In the following pages we have selected and reclassified some of these hoary devices to fit into a modern context and have added a few devices for which the original Greek terms have eluded us. All of these—illustrated with examples—can be used to make your own expression more powerful.

FIGURES OF SPEECH

TROPE

A STRIKING OR UNUSUAL ARRANGEMENT OF WORDS IS A "FIG-ure of speech." During the eighteenth century, these were named tropes or turns and were divided into two groups: There were difficult ornaments (which most of us have learned to call figures of speech), and easy ornaments or schemes (which we have retermed figures of structure). The "difficult" ornaments include ten basic tropes and some extensions.

Essentially, trope is a device that changes the meanings of words. For this, Cicero used the term "figure" if the meaning of more than one word was changed. Quintilian and Bede emphasized that it was the change in significance of the word rather than in the meaning that created the trope—that the term "figure" was a change in the forms of a scheme or structure of a sentence. For most rhetoricians, trope includes the metaphor, the simile, metonymy, synecdoche, icon, hyperbole, personification, antonomasia, irony, analogy, and variations of these. In each generation there have been those who reclassified, redefined, renamed, and redivided the groups so that there are perhaps a thousand names for tropes. Typically:

Windshield wipers applauding in the rain.

—Eric Sevareid

. . . time is the longest distance between two places.
—Tennessee Williams

He mounts the storm, and walks upon the wind.
—Alexander Pope

THE METAPHOR

The best known and most widely used of the tropes is the metaphor. To create a metaphor, you change the literal meaning of a word or phrase or idea to reproduce an image or an idea more effectively. You create a metaphor by bringing together two phenomena—ideas, images, events, or things—simultaneously, so that some or all of the properties of one are transferred to the other. This transference, this change of perspective, makes a comparison by substitution. Almost all of us use metaphors in our everyday speech automatically. The advantage of a metaphor is its ability to be more precise than an adjective, and, often, to carry an emotional impact.

The word *metaphor* itself comes from the Greek "transference" (Puttenham called metaphor *transport*); metaphor has the property of changing the literal meaning of a word to an analogous, nonliteral meaning. (The Greek *meta* means beyond and *phero* means to bear or carry.) It is shorter than the simile because it does not contain the words *like* or *as*. It asserts an identity rather than the "likeness" of the simile. Aristotle gave a memorable characterization: "Midway between the unintelligible and the commonplace, it is the metaphor which most produces knowledge." Quintilian saw it as a short simile, "the most beautiful of tropes providing a name for everything."

Metaphor involves two elements: One is *epiphor* (Aristotle's word for transference), of which the best element calls attention to similarities not readily noticed. The other is *diaphor*, the transference of aspects of real or imagined experience. One commentator gives this example of bringing together diverse elements to create a new emotional impact:

My country 'tis of thee
Sweet land of liberty
Higgledy-piggledy my black hen

The antipatriotic verse juxtaposes two ordinary expressions to create a radical, entirely unrelated impression. Gertrude Stein uses a diaphoric approach with:

Toasted Susie is my ice cream

In your own work you might try these six ancient functions of metaphor:

1. To increase vividness:

Rows of well mannered poplars escorted the road to the city.

Jonquils awaken in surprise with snowflakes melting in their eyes.

He is the only case of a bull who carries his China closet with him.

—Winston Churchill

2. For brevity:

the wind has a beveled edge.

what a Bedlamite is man

—John Adams

3. To avoid obscenity:

The wrongs of love, like the notes of a solvent debtor bear interest.

—Honoré de Balzac

4. For magnifying:

In Israel, in order to be a realist, you must believe in miracles.

—David Ben-Gurion

5. For minimizing:

. . . the general look of an elderly fallen angel traveling incognito.

—Peter Quenell of André Gide

6. For embellishing:

The Wright Brothers flew right through the smoke screen of impossibility.

—Charles Franklin Kettering

You may also employ an emotional element, pleasant, or unpleasant, as well as the image that is carried:

Say it with flowers!

In the cathedral of my heart, a candle was always burning for you.

—S. N. Behrman

Or a negative feeling:

Vice, like desire, floats in the atmosphere.

—William Hazlitt

WHAT MAKES A METAPHOR GOOD

Your metaphor is best when it is not too obvious, but not so enigmatic as to be obscure. The effectiveness of a metaphor varies directly with its unexpectedness, and therefore with its originality. A genuine metaphor is striking because it stimulates the mind of your reader or listener to find the relationships and to realize two meanings simultaneously.

There are standard cautions on the use of metaphor in all its varieties. It must be appropriate to the audience, to the subject, and to the style. Metaphors used in a close context should be consistent with each other; mixed metaphors are confusing—almost illiterate, but likely to come naturally:

We'll try to iron out the bottlenecks.

Now that Jim is back in the saddle, everything will be smooth sailing.

No one is above the fault of mixed metaphors:

. . . to take arms against a sea of troubles . . .
—William Shakespeare

If you let that sort of thing go on, your bread and butter will be cut out from under your feet.
—Aneurin Bevan

Thus Sadat wrestled with the Devil for the soul of Egypt, and lost, because the Devil had most of the cards, and the jury of world opinion was half asleep and wholly blinkered.
—Max Lerner

Paper tigers don't take the lion's share.
—*San Francisco Chronicle-San Francisco Examiner*

If your metaphor is too grand or too farfetched it appears ridiculous. And it must not be a worn-out expression—widely used before. The metaphor cries out to be original. As the metaphor is used again and again, it becomes trite and dead, a cliché: "dead as a doornail," "packed like sardines," "white as a sheet," "busy as a bee," "a storm of protest," "a flight of fancy," "a ray of hope," "no axe to grind," "shoulder to the wheel," "hair-raising experience," "didn't raise a finger," "keeping in step."

As is evident, clichés are not limited to figures of speech, epigrams, or quotations. The fault may exist in the repetition of stock phrases and the use of overworked ideas. However, you can make an allusion to a cliché to take it out of the worn-out state. Thus Galsworthy has a character say:

Come . . . milk's spilt.

and again!

You know which side the law's buttered.

Here are some original uses of the metaphor:

Faith goes up the stairs that love has made and looks out of the windows which hope has opened.
                                        —Charles H. Spurgeon

. . . man is still the most extraordinary computer of all.
                                        —John F. Kennedy, honoring astronaut
                                        L. Gordon Cooper, Jr.

Time is but the stream I go a-fishing in.
                                        —Henry David Thoreau

Hitch your wagon to a star.
                                        —Ralph Waldo Emerson

People who've had a hanging in the family don't like to talk about a rope.
                                        —Calvin Coolidge

I somehow feel there's a boomerang loose in the room.
                                        —Charles E. Wilson, on ducking questions
                                        at a news conference

THE METAPHOR EXTENDED

Metaphor may be even more effective when you extend its use from a simple phrase to a series of related images. Thus:

Mr. Dombey's cup of satisfaction was so full at this moment, however, that he felt he could afford a drop or two of its contents, even to sprinkle on the dust in the by-path of his little daughter.
                                        —Charles Dickens

. . . the flames kindled on the 4th of July, 1776, have spread over too much of the globe to be extinguished by the feeble engines of despotism; on the contrary, they will consume these engines and all who work them. . . .
                                        —Thomas Jefferson in a letter to John Adams

He came into my life as the warm wind of spring had awakened flowers, as the April showers awaken the earth. My love for him was an unchanging love, high and deep, free and faithful, strong as death. Each year I learned to love him more and more. . . .
> —Anna Chennault of her romance and marriage
> to U.S. General Claire Chennault

. . . You shall not press down upon the brow of labor this crown of thorns. You shall not crucify mankind upon a cross of gold.
> —William Jennings Bryan

Some books are to be tasted, others to be swallowed, and some few to be chewed and digested.
> —Francis Bacon

That's one small step for a man, one giant leap for mankind.
> —Astronaut Neil Armstrong, first words
> spoken on the moon broadcast to Earth

VARIATIONS OF METAPHOR

Rhetoricians have distinguished variations of metaphor—and through the years described these in a potpourri of classifications, each subtly different from the others.

There is the kind of metaphor that the Greeks called *catachresis*, meaning "misapplication," and the Romans called *abusio*, meaning "abuse." The term is applied to the far-fetched or extreme metaphor, which is not necessarily inappropriate.

I will speak daggers to her.
> —William Shakespeare, *Hamlet*

. . . earrings like chandeliers . . .
> —William Makepeace Thackeray

What an ocean is life! And how our barks get separated in beating through it.

—Thomas Jefferson

Poetry is the impish attempt to paint the color of the wind.

—Maxwell Bodenheim

. . . this capital city of high-tension activity.

—Stanley Levey, *The New York Times*

My God, in this job, he's got the nerve of a burglar.

—President Kennedy, of Adlai Stevenson
as UN Ambassador, *Time*

A few hair shirts are part of the mental wardrobe of every man. The President differs from other men only in that he has a more extensive wardrobe.

—Herbert Hoover

The trouble with our age is that it is all signposts and no destination.

—Louis Kronenberger

When you substitute one part of speech for another part of speech, the metaphor is termed *anthimeria*, from the Greek "one part for another." Thus you may replace a noun with an adjective, a verb with an adverb, often providing a more descriptive and vivid image. A similar device known as *enallage*, from the Greek "interchange," sometimes also called changeling ("exchange"), involves the substitution of one case, person, tense, number, mood, or part of speech for another.

His complexion is perfect gallows.

—William Shakespeare

Earth laughs in flowers.

—Ralph Waldo Emerson

. . . in the evening of my memory I come back to West Point.
Always there echoes and re-echoes: duty, honor, country.
—Douglas MacArthur, at West Point

THE SIMILE

The metaphor is a compressed simile. To create a well-recognized simile, you specifically compare unlike things, usually with the use of the words "like" or "as" or "is." It is not usually as subtle, and it is much more limited in imagery than the metaphor.

The distinction between metaphor and simile is largely ignored by writers. But basically, compared to a metaphor, there is more directness, more casualness in simile. Some variations:

As welcome as a letter from home.

Sir, you are like a pin, but without either its head or its point.
—Douglas Jerold to a speaker who
was boring him

Hearts that click like taximeters.

[He] had a face like a benediction.
—Miguel de Cervantes Saavedra

Venice is like eating an entire box of chocolate liqueurs in one go.
—Truman Capote

He keeps himself in the public eye like a cinder.

He finds fault as if it were a buried treasure.
—F. O. Walsh

The New York Times uses simile to lighten a business story:

Last September, in a silence almost as loud as the fanfare in which it was introduced, Micrin was taken off the market.

Your similes may of course be more extensive:

The man who has not anything to boast of but his illustrious ancestors is like a potato, the only good belonging of his is underground.

—Sir Thomas Overbury

Scoops of mint ice cream with chips of chocolate cows.

—Jim Bishop, *of the English countryside*

Publishing a volume of verse is like dropping a rose petal down the Grand Canyon and waiting for the echo.

—Don Marquis

In a universe whose size is beyond human imagining where our world floats like a dust mote in the void of night, men have grown inconceivably lonely.

—Loren Eiseley

Or in a political situation:

Treaties are like roses and young girls. They last while they last.

—Charles de Gaulle

Yes! Like the grub that feeds on the Royal Jelly and thinks it's a Queen Bee.

—Winston Churchill, of Prime Minister
Clement Attlee who succeeded him

The Democrats ought to win it, but the Republicans think they can pull it out, and the outlook is for a race as tight as a cowboy's Levi's.

—*The New York Times*

Your simile may involve only a verb:

Power is poison.

—Henry Adams

. . . closer together than the hands of a clock at twenty minutes of eight.

—Robert Bedingfield, of the brothers
John Murchison and Clint Murchison, Jr.

It can be presented as an equation or a comparison:

What garlic is to salad, insanity is to art.

—Augustus Saint-Gaudens

Money is like manure. If you spread it around, it does a lot of good, but if you pile it up in one place, it stinks like hell.

—Clint Murchison, Jr., Texas financier

A reverse twist provides a refreshing variation:

Heaven is a Kentucky of a place.

—Kentucky guidebook

THE SIMILE EXTENDED

Antapodosis, from the Greek "giving back in return," is a simile in which you extend the comparison in several respects. The Romans called it *redditio contraria*:

There is a recurring tendency on the part of the press and the public to view a Presidential campaign as a cross between a beauty contest and a tennis match. It is like a beauty contest in that the candidates are judged on their physical endowments such as their smiles, their profiles and their hair; and like a tennis match, they are judged on their acquired skills such as speechmaking and news conference technique.

—*The New York Times*

Thurber did not write the way a surgeon operates; he wrote the way a child skips rope, the way a mouse waltzes.

—E. B. White

Fame is a bee.
It has a song—

It has a sting—
Ah, too, it has a wing.

—Emily Dickinson

His face had the beery, bruised appearance of the continual drinker's; it was covered with a network of congested veins, purple in ordinary circumstances but now pale violet, for even with his back to the fire, the cold pinched him on the other side.

—Robert Louis Stevenson

There is nothing like the ticker tape except a woman—nothing that promises, hour after hour, day after day, such sudden developments; nothing that disappoints so often or occasionally fulfills with such unbelievable, passionate magnificence.

—Walter Knowlegon Gutman

Energy in a nation is like sap in a tree; it rises from the bottom up; it does not come from the top down. . . . When I was a schoolmaster, I used to say that the trouble about the college sophomore was that the sap of manhood was rising in him, but hadn't reached his head.

—Woodrow Wilson

Here's to women: So much like a clock—pretty hands, pretty face, pretty movement, and hard to regulate when they get out of order.

—Arthur L. Kaser

METONYMY

Metonymy (me-TON-ih-mee) is derived from the Greek "change of name." Rhetoricians have variously called it *denominatio, transnominatio, transmutation,* and Puttenham, *misnamer.* For this figure you substitute cause for effect, the effect for the cause, or use an attribute or a proper name instead of the literal meaning. In other words, you substitute one thing for another with which it is associated. The analogous suggests the word. You may create metonymy:

1. By substituting a concrete image for an abstract idea: "Blood is thicker than water."

2. By substituting the container for the contents: "He is addicted to the bottle."

3. By substituting a place for an act: "He met his Waterloo."

4. By substituting the material for the object: "He is a man of the cloth."

5. By substituting a specific tool for a larger concept: "You can't dig coal with bayonets."

Metonymy is different from metaphor because it is not based on transfer of qualities, but by association of part for the whole: the gun for the military or war, the cup for the drink, the grape for wine, the red cap for the cardinal, 10 Downing Street for the government, and so forth. Thus:

> Miss Tox's hand trembled as she slipped it through Mr. Dombey's arm, and felt herself escorted up the steps, *preceded by a cocked hat and a Babylonian collar.*
>
> —Charles Dickens

And again, Dickens:

> There was something so very agreeable in being so intimate with such a *waistcoat*; in being on such off-hand terms so soon with such *a pair of whiskers* that Tom was uncommonly pleased with himself.

> Our national flower is the concrete cloverleaf.
>
> —Lewis Mumford

> Take things always by their smooth handle.
>
> —Thomas Jefferson

> The years teach much which the days never know.
>
> —Ralph Waldo Emerson

> Her hair was mouse brown, with a tendency to scamper.
>
> —Ellery Queen

It may be extended:

Summer is a sailor in a rowboat and ice-cream on your dress when you're four years old. Summer is a man with his coat off, wet sand between your toes, the smell of a garden an hour before moonrise. Oh summer is silk itself, a giant geranium and music from a flute far away.

—Michael Brown

In practice, you may extend metonymy to anything associated with the original thought. One authority on rhetoric lists it as one of the four major tropes, with metaphor, synecdoche, and irony. Often the distinction is subtle.

SYNECDOCHE

Synecdoche (pronounced sin-NECK-doe-key) is understanding one thing when we say another: a part for a whole, a species for a genus. It has been an accepted rhetorical technique for almost two millennia. Romans called it *intellectio*; Puttenham called it *quick conceite*. It is broader in concept than metonymy. A simple use is: "All hands on deck."

Synecdoche as a figure of speech received great publicity when the Senate Select Committee on Intelligence, in November 1976, reported on alleged assassination plots by agencies of the United States government. According to that report, the agencies used synecdoche to shroud their sinister intentions in ambiguity. The device was "the mention of a part when the whole was to be understood." As a result, the report concludes, there was a "failure of communications" between CIA and the policy makers. There were "differing interpretations of such orders as 'dispose of Castro,' 'remove Castro,' and 'knock off Castro.'" To some interpreters this meant "overthrow the Communist government in Cuba" or "do something about Castro."

In literature and more prosaic communications, synecdoche is a common device.

Two notable drawbacks of civilization; a palace . . . and soldiers.

—George Bernard Shaw

The way to a man's heart is through his stomach.

A chicken in every pot, a car in every garage.

—Republican slogan in 1932

We must be the great arsenal of democracy.

—Franklin D. Roosevelt

With the supermarket as our temple and the singing commercial as our litany, are we likely to fire the world with an irresistible vision of America's exalted purposes and inspiring way of life?

—Adlai Stevenson

A contemporary use applies synecdoche to logic:

Within the vast mass of poverty that is India there is a sizeable modern economy, comprising 10% or more of the Indian population, or 50 million people.

—Peter Drucker

Or a simple bit of humor:

They tell me he fell in love with a pair of blue eyes—then he made the mistake of marrying the whole girl.

—Joey Adams

ICON

Icon—translated as likeness, image, or portrait—is from the Greek and is widely used, but less often noted. Here you put the accent on imagery: You delineate a person or an object.

Office buildings like upended ice trays.

—Stanley Elkin

. . . this great asparagus bed of alabaster and rose and green skyscrapers.

—Cecil Beaton

Her neck was like a stately tower.

—Thomas Lode

. . . a baby's dainty bouquet of pink toes.

—Dorothy Hoffman

An unnerving squeal went up, like forty thousand Persian cats having their tails trodden on simultaneously.

—*Manchester Guardian* of a female audience responding to a Liberace appearance

HYPERBOLE

Hyperbole—from the Greek "excess exaggeration"—involves the use of extravagant terms or comparisons that are not to be taken literally. Every child and every fisherman has used it. The Romans labeled it *superlatio*; Puttenham called it descriptively *loud lyer* and *overreacher*. Thus Pope's description of a lion:

> He roared so loud, and looked so
> wondrous grim,
> His very shadow durst not follow him.

Hyperbole is not, of course, mere exaggeration: It is intended to be understood as exaggeration either to make a point or to suggest an emotional response.

Hyperbole is commonly used in inexact conversations. Jimmy Durante's response to applause was "I gotta million of 'em." Mark Antony did not, of course, mean it literally, when he announced, "Let Rome in Tiber melt, and the wide arch of the rang'd empire fall!" when he protested his love for Cleopatra. Traditionally, romance is built on such hyperbole. Justin Hunt Maccarthy created a dramatic tribute to his lady:

If I were king
What tributary nations would I bring,
To stoop before your sceptre and to swear
Allegiance to your lips, and eyes, and hair
Beneath your feet what treasures would I fling.
The stars would be your pearls upon a string,
The world a ruby for your finger ring,
And you should have the sun and moon to wear
If I were king.

and listen to:

I expect to fight that proposition until hell freezes over. Then I propose to start fighting on the ice.
> —Senator Russell Long of Louisiana on President Kennedy's request for a cutoff of funds to areas practicing segregation

Australian humor is heavily spiced with exaggeration and gentle leg pulling.

One cattleman told another, "It was so cold in our town that the candle light froze and we couldn't blow it out." The other said, "That's nothing, mate. Where we were the words came out of our mouth in pieces of ice, and we had to fry them to see what we were talking about."

A classic is:

He could sell iceboxes to Eskimos.

believed to have originated in the Yukon during the Gold Rush in the late 1890s.

Here are some other suggestive examples:

I tell you how cold it's been; I passed a statue of Napoleon, and he had both hands inside his jacket.
> —Credited to Jesse Kaplan by Earl Wilson

He and I had an office so tiny that an inch smaller and it would have been adultery.
—Dorothy Parker, on sharing space at
Vanity Fair with Robert Benchley

He was so tall that I was not sure he had a face.
—Mark Twain

Hyperbole is the stuff on which advertising flourishes:

At sixty miles an hour the loudest noise in the new Rolls-Royce comes from the electric clock.
—Rolls-Royce advertisement

When you're perfect people can't wait to pick you apart.
—Paramount chickens

The Maytag repairman is the loneliest man in the world.

Introducing Xerox 9400 . . . Will miracles never cease.

THE EPITHET

Technically the epithet is an attributive word, phrase, or sentence that characterizes an object. It is more than a simple adjective, like "green eyes," which describes a quality generally recognized. Here you must use a subjective description: "piercing eyes" or "tearing eyes" or "loving eyes." The epithet carries an emotional impact rather than being merely descriptive. As a result you may often use a hyphenated adjective: "cat-like eyes," or a made-to-order combination:

There is a sort of "Oh-what-a-wicked-world-this-is-and-how-I-wish-I-could-do-something-to-make-it-better-and-nobler" expression about Montmorency that has been known to bring the tears into the eyes of pious old ladies and gentlemen.
—Jerome K. Jerome in *Three Men in a Boat*

Here it is used in an advertisement:

Another ho-hum run-yourself-ragged, 12-hour day without dictating equipment.
How long can you hold out?

—Lanier Business Products

Or you may use a whole series of piled-up adjectives (which the Greeks called *congeries*). This is from O. Henry's description of New York City:

Such was the background of the wonderful, cruel, enchanting, bewildering, fatal, great city.

and this from an advertisement in London underground trains, "with acknowledgements to Roget."

Good, excellent, superior, above par, nice, fine, choice, rare, priceless, unparagoned, unparalleled, superfine, superexcellent, of the first water, crack, prime, tip-top, gilt-edged, first-class, capital, cardinal, couleur de rose, peerless, matchless, inestimable, precious as the apple of the eye, satisfactory, fair, fresh, unspoiled, sound; GKN: over 80 companies making steel and steel products.

—Guest, Kan, & Nettlefolds, Ltd.

PERSONIFICATION

Personification was one of the most popular of the tropes in the eighteenth and nineteenth centuries. It was called *prosopopoeia* by the Greeks, *conformatio* ("symmetrical forming") by the Romans, and *counterfait impersonation* by Puttenham. The same term applies to quoting an imaginary person. There are various ways of using it.

Most common is attributing a human quality to an abstract or inanimate object. Thus, Washington was "the Father of his country."

The soft underbelly of the Axis.

—Winston Churchill

Falsehoods not only disagree with truths, but usually quarrel among themselves.

—Daniel Webster

Imagination is the eye of the soul!

—Petrus Jacobus Joubert

Lose an hour in the morning, and you will be all day hunting for it.

—Richard Whately

Caution is the eldest child of wisdom.

—Victor Hugo

Money swore an oath that nobody that did not love it should ever have it.

—Irish proverb

Boys are the cash of war. Whoever said we're not free spenders doesn't know our likes.

—John Ciardi

A tree changes her robe to green.

In advertising:

In tonight's martini the part of gin and vodka will be played by white rum.

—Puerto Rican Rum

Bacon with "good morning" in every slice.

—Rath Meals

The qualities of animals are sometimes cited.

The fog comes on little cat feet.

—Carl Sandburg

ANTONOMASIA

A variation of personification is *antonomasia*, the Greek for "to name instead." It has also been called *pronominatio*,

nominatio, and, by Puttenham, *surnamer*. By using a proper name—sometimes by using a descriptive phrase for a proper name—you describe a quality associated with that name. Calling someone a Quisling, a Benedict Arnold, or a little Napoleon are common uses. The rhetorician Quintilian saw in it a resemblance to synecdoche. Some names already are part of our vocabulary: Dunkirk is an evacuation of troops under fire to avoid catastrophe; Waterloo is a last defeat; a Don Juan is a philanderer.

> A vile race of quislings—to use a new word which will carry the scorn of mankind down the centuries.
>
> —Winston Churchill

You can attain a slightly different effect by what the Greeks called *prosonomasia* (for "nickname") and Puttenham called *nicknamer*. Here you apply the name of a person to a trait for which he or she was known. Thus of the Emperor of Ethiopia, "The Lion of Judah," and similarly Alfred the Great, Stonewall Jackson, Ivan the Terrible.

Antonomasia is a device that depends on the interplay between the nominal meaning of a word and the logical meaning. You create a token name for a characteristic—sometimes with, sometimes without an explanation. In the seventeenth, eighteenth, and even nineteenth centuries many if not most characters in plays and novels were characterized by their names: Ben Jonson's characters bore such names as Lady Would-be, Master Damplay, Truewit, and Winwife. In Lord Byron's *Don Juan* there are: Sir John Pottledeep, the mighty drinker; the sage Miss Reading; two fair co-heiresses with the name of Giltbedding; Dick Dubious who loves philosophy; Sir Henry Silvercup, the race winner.

In a reverse approach, you may describe the abstract as a person:

> Society is now one polish'd horde,
> Formed of two mighty tribes, the Bores
> and Bored.
>
> —George Gordon Lord Byron, *Don Juan*

From the London *Times*:

I say this to our American friends, Mr. Facing-Both-Ways does not get very far in this world.

Frailty, thy name is woman!
—William Shakespeare

When I was a young man I courted Popularity. I found her but a coy mistress, and I soon deserted her . . .
—John Adams

I don't want to see the Republican Party ride to political victory on the Four Horsemen of Calumny—Fear, Ignorance, Bigotry and Smear.
—Margaret Chase Smith

When brooding Darkness spreads his jealous wings . . .
—John Milton

It would be folly to ignore that we live in a motor age. . . . It long ago ran down Simple Living, and never halted to inquire about the prostrate figure which fell as its victim.
—Warren G. Harding

And Freedom shriek'd—as Kosciusko fell!
—Thomas Campbell

Public discussion is helping to doom slavery. What kills a skunk is the publicity it gives itself.
—Abraham Lincoln

Advertisers use the device in naming products:

Taster's Choice, Nice 'n' Easy

IRONY

Irony is the negative form of metaphor. It uses two meanings—one from the dictionary, the other from the context—to say the opposite of what appears to be said: Irony is often the product of a situation or a series of circumstances. Much more is made of it in our description of negative figures. (See pages 140–165.)

The disparity between what is said and what is meant provides the effectiveness of the irony.

Asked in Parliament about Britain's protection against atom bomb attack, Winston Churchill answered:

> The honorable member must not, in his innocence, take the bread from the mouths of the Soviet Secret Service.

And at another time, Churchill noted:

> He has the greatest opportunity for public service. He can resign today.

ANALOGY

Analogy has many meanings in rhetoric. For our purpose, we select "the comparison of situations." The word itself is from the Greek meaning "equality of ratios." The Romans called it *proportio*. Here are some modern applications:

> None preaches better than the ant, and she says nothing.
> —Benjamin Franklin

> You have offered to trade us an apple for an orchard. We do not do that in this country.
> —President Kennedy, on Berlin, to
> Soviet Foreign Minister Andrei Gromyko

> The notion that disarmament can put a stop to war is contradicted by the nearest dog fight.
> —George Bernard Shaw

> If it is a crime to make a counterfeit dollar, it is ten thousand times worse to make a counterfeit man.
> —Abraham Lincoln

Following the lines of least resistance makes men and rivers crooked.

—Ralph Pierce

Every man's life is a fairytale written by God's fingers.

—Hans Christian Andersen

. . . What is good for the country is good for General Motors, and vice versa.

—Charles E. Wilson, President of General Motors

A man who could make so vile a pun would not scruple to pick a pocket.

—John Dennis, *The Gentleman's Magazine*

It would indeed be the ultimate tragedy if the history of the human race proved to be nothing more noble than the story of an ape playing with a box of matches on a petrol dump.

—David Ormsby Gore

In the old days we used to say that when the United States economy sneezed the rest of the world went to bed with pneumonia. Now when the United States economy sneezes the other countries say "Gesundheit."

—Walter Heller

The cure for bad politics is the same as the cure for tuberculosis. It is the living in the open.

—Woodrow Wilson

Govern a great nation as you would cook a small fish. [Don't overdo it.]

—Lao-Tze

Fish and visitors smell in three days.

—Benjamin Franklin

Administering a college today is like playing chess on the open deck of the sinking Titanic . . .

—Dr. Edward Bloustein

Fun is like life insurance; the older you get, the more it costs.
—Frank McKinney Hubbard

Habits are at first cobwebs, then cables.
—Spanish proverb

This country has come to feel the same when Congress is in session as when the baby gets hold of a hammer.
—Will Rogers

Learn to say "no." It will be of more use to you than to be able to read Latin.
—Charles H. Spurgeon

With all the confidence of a man dialing his own telephone number . . .
—Jack Bell of Robert A. Taft

It's like getting a shave and having your appendix out at the same time.
—Robert Lovett, on exigencies of being Secretary of Defense

This idea that you can merchandise candidates for high office like breakfast cereal—that you can gather votes like box tops— is, I think, the ultimate indignity to the democratic process.
—Adlai Stevenson

I am rather like a mosquito in a nudist camp; I know what I ought to do, but I don't know where to begin.
—Stephen Bayne, on assuming a new post

THE FABLE

It was the Greeks who gave us Aesop, and they also had a term for the fable: *apologue*, sometimes called *aenos*, which translates as "story." Actually, it is the wise sayings from these stories, rather than the stories themselves, which they considered the apologue. Modern writing accepts the story with the point—usually a moral point—as a fable. Like the ancient writers, you may use animal characters, but humans will serve as well.

Once upon a time a horse and a donkey were taken on the same trip by their master. The donkey, who carried all the supplies, said to the horse, "if you would take a share of my load, it would save my life." But the horse refused to help, and it was not long before the donkey was worn out with fatigue and fell down and died. Then the owner took all the supplies off the donkey's back and put them on the horse's back, plus the hide of the donkey. Then the horse began to complain saying, "Look at me now. I wouldn't take the light load when I had a chance and now I must carry everything—including the donkey."

—Aesop

THE ALLEGORY, THE PARABLE

The *allegory* is somewhat different. The term comes from the Greek meaning "speaking otherwise than one seems to speak" and was at various times called *inversio* and (by Puttenham) *false semblant*. To use this device, you extend a metaphor through a complete unit—creating a sustained metaphor. For "pure allegory," every element should be congruent in its double significance. The definition in literary criticism is much broader than that applied in rhetoric; the characters represent things or ideas.

A parable is a story that could happen. Puttenham called the device *resemblance misticall*.

Once upon a time there was a little girl who always said "thank you" at birthday parties; who called friends of the family Aunt Helen and Uncle Jim; and who passed out free cookies the day her lemonade stand opened. When this little girl grew up she didn't go to heaven. She went into public relations, and learned that what to her had always been unconscious art is now classified as a science—the engineering of consent—worth a hundred a week to her and millions in good will to her clients.

—Mary Ann Gintor, *The Million Dollar Science,* 1956

Once upon a time there was a man who became wise. He learned not to make a single gesture which was not useful. Soon afterward he was shut up.

—Paul Valéry

EXAMPLES

Exemplum, a sample, at one time called *paradigma,* may be either true or feigned. To relate a story about a great or an ordinary person is a common way to use this device.

An ancient tablet tells of a prophet who vowed to learn the secret of life without food. Just as he was learning to live without eating—he died.

A citizen of ancient Rome sought to divorce his wife, and as a result was severely chastened by his friends, who asked: "Was she not chaste? Was she not fair?" The Roman held out one of his shoes. "Is it not well made?" he said. "Is it not also new?" And when they agreed that the shoe was both well made and new, the Roman replied: "Yet none of you can tell where it pinches me."

—Plutarch

THE ANECDOTE

The anecdote is a short, entertaining account of an incident, or a little-known fact, and is most often personal. An example is the toastmaster's "story with a point," designed principally to break the ice with the audience. Similarly, as a writer you can sometimes use it to hook your reader at the beginning of an essay or article.

Someone asked me, as I came down the street, how I felt. I was reminded of a story that a fellow townsman of ours used to tell about Abraham Lincoln. They asked him how he felt once after an unsuccessful election. He said he felt like a little boy who had stubbed his toe in the dark; that he was too old to cry, but it hurt too much to laugh.

—Adlai Stevenson

IV

FIGURES OF SOUND AND SIGHT

AURAL DEVICES

WHEN WE THINK OF WRITING, WE ASSOCIATE IT WITH READing—silent reading. But much writing is designed for oral delivery. Until a hundred years ago, most popular communication was oral—in the Middle Ages from a troubadour or a storyteller and, later, from the dais or the pulpit. Even today, as we read silently, we auralize—we hear the sounds of words in our mind's ear. Although we may never utter the words aloud, alliteration, assonance, onomatopeia are registered with us. Thus not only good speakers but also good writers are concerned with how their words sound.

Not only can words come tripping off the tongue, but they can carry a message beyond the definition of the words themselves. This often makes the communication more penetrating, more easily remembered, and more readily repeated.

Of the aural devices, rhythm is most common in all phases of writing and speaking. Rhythm alone makes some writings so distinctive that the reader is able to identify the writer from a single paragraph. Iambic rhythm made the invectives of Archilochus synonymous with bitter satire for centuries, and more complex rhythms have been valuable tools for writers and speakers ever since.

The word rhythm comes from the Greek *rhuthmos*, a measured movement, akin to *rhein*, to flow. Natural rhythm flows in the nervous system of everyone. "We grow up in rhythm," Louis Untermeyer once said. "We feel it physically in the breath, the pulse and the heartbeat; we measure it in our walking stride; we quicken to it in the sway of the dance. We feel it psychologically—we are lulled by the swing of a hammock; we are excited by the beat of a drum; what Emily Dickinson called 'the accent of a coming foot' fills us with anticipation and apprehension."

One way of expressing rhythms is through verse. The poet articulates responses and emotions by giving them form. Rhythm, in effect, sets off images in which movement creates forms in time.

Ninety-five percent of verse in English up to the mid-twentieth century is written in iambic rhythm. Iambic verse is essentially alternating rhythm; every other syllable is stressed. As you read the first few lines of a poem aloud to yourself, suppressing any impulse you might have to give certain syllables more emphasis than they receive naturally, the rhythm becomes apparent.

> Shall I compare thee to a summer's day?
> Thou art more lovely and more temperate:
> Rough winds do shake the darling buds of May,
> And summer's lease hath all too short a date:
> —William Shakespeare

As you read, you notice that the pitch, duration, and vowel and consonant sounds differ in each syllable. These differences between the sounds of certain syllables are differences of stress. While you are listening to the rhythm, there is a general pattern of sound that needs to be recognized as well. This pattern of sound is *meter*. Ignore the differences between the syllables and see what they have in common. These similarities are the *accents*.

To discover a metrical pattern, scan the poem. Scanning is

a way of indicating the type of pattern that is used in a poem. Poetry is scanned by a symbolic notation. The basic symbols in the scansion of poetry are x, indicating an unstressed syllable, and the /, indicating a fully stressed syllable, and \, indicating a slurring, as making three syllables into two. Sprung verse and free verse do not lend themselves to scansion.

x /	x /	x /	x /	x /	x /
Tis hard	to say	if grea	ter want	of skill	appear

x /	x \	x /	x /
in wri	ting or	in judg	ing ill.

A *foot* is a group of two or three syllables. In the line below, each foot is composed of two syllables, the line of ten feet. Thus:

1	2	3	4	5	6	7	8	9	10
Shall I		com	pare	thee	to	a	sum	mer's	day?

The types of feet in any given poem are usually:

Iamb: one short, or unaccented syllable, followed by one long, or accented syllable (u/)

Trochee: one long, or accented syllable, followed by one short, or unaccented syllable (/u)

Anapest: two short, or unaccented syllables, followed by one long, or accented syllable (uu/)

Dactyl: one long, or accented syllable, followed by two short, or unaccented syllables (/uu)

Spondee: two long, or accented syllables (//)

The first line of this sonnet is therefore described as five iambs:

u /	u /	u /	u /	u /
Shall I	compare	thee to	a sum	mer's day?

We describe the number of feet in each line thus:

Monometer: one foot
Dimeter: two feet
Trimeter: three feet

Tetrameter: four feet
Pentameter: five feet
Hexameter: six feet

Inasmuch as the lines analyzed contain five iambs, the metrical pattern of the poem is described as an iambic pentameter. Iambic pentameter is the most common metrical form in English verse and often finds its way into English prose. The major difference between free verse and metrical verse is that there is no regular number of feet in each line of free verse.

Here is a rhythmic look at a piece of prose from Abraham Lincoln's second inaugural address. It can also be rearranged into lines to indicate that its rhythm is that of a slightly irregular lyric.

```
 /    x  x  x    /
Fondly  do  we  hope

 /   x  x   x x   /
Fervently  do  we  pray

 x    x  /  x   /      x  /
That  this  mighty  scourge  of  war

  x   /  xx    /    x/
May  speedily  pass  away.
```

In ordinary prose, rhythm that is so regular as to call attention to itself defeats its purpose. It distracts from the meaning of the sentence. Prose should not be scanned on the same critical basis as poetry.

Rhythm is an element understood by almost everyone but difficult to define. It is not just meter. Quintilian calls it "a system of time intervals arranged according to a given order." However, some rhythms have no time association. Another definition calls it "a repetition of the same, or a very similar, sensory element or group of elements." More important than definition is what rhythm does: It stirs up emotions—through words and design.

In poetry two rhythmic elements appear: one based on time (length of syllables) the other based on accent (or loudness). In English, the length of vowels plays an important part.

> When you were a tadpole and
> I was a fish in the Palaeozoic time
> And side by side in the sluggish tide, we
> sprawled in the ooze and slime.
>
> —Langdon Smith, *Evolution*

In ordinary prose writing, the pattern of rhythm is "an affair of the paragraph." In this way it is so widely dispersed as to be unnoticed and almost unidentifiable. The perception of rhythm becomes an unconscious appreciation. Utilizing figures of structure described in the next chapter provides a medium for rhythm in prose. Most good writing has a rhythm in structure and often in thought that helps readability, understanding, impact, and facility to be remembered.

Cicero made much of this rhythm: "The ear, or the mind through the ear, contains in itself a certain natural measure of all spoken sounds." Swing with this paragraph from Woodrow Wilson's momentous address asking for United States entry into the First World War, April 2, 1917:

> To such a task we dedicate our lives, our fortunes, everything that we are and everything that we have, with the pride of those who know that the day has come when America is privileged to spend her blood and her might for the principles that gave her birth and happiness and the peace which she has treasured. God helping her, she can do no other.

Or this from Abraham Lincoln's second inaugural address in 1865:

> With malice toward none, with charity for all, with firmness in the right, as God gives us to see the right, let us strive on to finish the work we are in . . . to do all which may achieve

and cherish a just and lasting peace among ourselves, and with all nations.

Every American can identify with Thomas Jefferson's words:

> We hold these truths to be self-evident: that all men are created equal; that they are endowed by their creator with certain unalienable rights; that among these are life, liberty, and the pursuit of happiness. . . .

In a more ordinary circumstance, a dactylic hexameter is noted by *The New Yorker*:

> To remove the connector, push it in, turn to the left, and pull it off the terminal.

Basil Davenport ascribes to a physics textbook:

> And hence no force, however great, can draw a cord, however fine, into a horizontal line which shall be absolutely straight.

Occasionally rhythm carries an added dimension. In Edward Lear's poem "The Nutcrackers and the Sugar Tongs," the rhythm simulates the beat of galloping horses.

> They rode through the street, and they rode by the station,
>   They galloped away to the beautiful shore;
> In silence they rode, and "made no observation,"
>   Save this: "We will never go back any more!"
> And still you might hear, till they rode out of hearing,
>   The Sugar-tongs snap, and the Crackers say "crack!"
> Till far in the distance their forms disappearing,
>   They faded away.—And they never came back!

In "How the Water Comes Down at Ladose" by Robert Southey you can hear the monotonous roar of a waterfall:

> And nearing and clearing, . . .
> and falling and crawling and sprawling, . . .
> and gleaming and streaming and steaming and beaming, . . .
> and in this way the water comes down at Ladose.

RHYME

Even more effective than rhythm as a mnemonic device is rhyme. Combined with rhythm it usually gives us the poem—or song. Before the printed word was for everyone, auditory mnemonics was the key element in propagandizing—through song, ballad, and liturgy. The pattern of rhyme and rhythm made the message—or story—easy to remember and to repeat.

Rhyme—a repetition of identical or closely similar sounds arranged at regular intervals—is an acoustical phenomenon made possible by three elements:

1/ Identity of accented vowels
2/ Identity of unaccented vowels
3/ Identity and identical order of consonants

The vowels in English are tone-clusters in which every partial tone has a specific pitch and intensity—"a" as in father, for example, has a frequency of vibrations between 1000 to 1300 per second. Thus each vowel has a musical equivalent. Memorable prose can, in this sense, be memorable music.

Not all rhyme is complete. Some rhymes vary in consonant, others in vowel sounds. These are incomplete rhymes, and they serve to provide additional variety. Thus: press, fresh, flesh; treble, trouble; worth, forth; tool, tale.

Dante (1265–1321) was the first true exponent of the theory of rhyme. He viewed it as associated with music, but he used it simply to communicate verbally.

The association of rhyme with meaning was developed in the nineteenth century by J. S. Scutze, a German. He concluded that the pleasure of rhyme results from the artistic ability of our mind to bring two different ideas under the control of one sound. Modern authority holds that rhyme produces an artistic effect, not because it invents an empty verbal echo to be mechanically reproduced between the two rows of words, but because it confronts and conveys different ideas through the harmony of identical sounds. The content is as important as the consonance.

Although rhyme was seldom used by ancient Greeks and Romans, theoretically rudimentary rhyme was known to Plato, even used by Gorgias, as in the rhymed prose climax to the famous speech by Agathon in Plato's "Symposium." Cicero (106–43 B.C.) and Quintilian (A.D. 35–100) were familiar with the device. They noticed different kinds of rhyme, of which the resemblance in grammatical endings was just a special case.

Aristotle (384–322 B.C.) mentions rhyme, which he calls *homoioteleuton* (Greek for "like ending") in his *Rhetoric*, when he writes of the structure and organization of "periods." He saw it as a variety of "making the extreme words of both members of a period like each other. . . ." This must happen either at the beginning or the end of each member, he said. At the beginning the whole word must bear the resemblance; "at the end the final syllables or inflections of the same word, or the same word repeated." All this helps us, he noted, "to devise lively and taking sayings."

Thus much early rhyme was not what we would define as rhyme today, but consisted of alliteration and assonance— which could occur at the beginning of words as well as at the end—or even simple repetition.

Strangely, rhyme did not come naturally to English. It was introduced into Europe by Goths and Huns and, being barbaric, was thought not worthy of use. Sometime before the English used it, rhyme appeared in medieval Latin in connection with choral singing in the Christian churches. From there it was introduced into vernacular verse, becoming characterized as poetry after 1300. Today rhyme need no longer be perfect (moon and loon) but is acceptable or even preferred if it is approximate (a poem by Emily Dickinson used "soul" and "at all"). Yet hardly any rhetorical device so invites remembering and repetition as rhyme. Is there an American who cannot readily learn:

All up and down the whole creation,
Sadly I roam,
Still longing for the old plantation,
and for the old folks at home.
—Stephen Foster, "The Old Folks at Home,"
(about 1851)

By the rude bridge that arched the flood,
Their flag to April's breeze unfurled,
Here once the embattled farmers stood,
And fired the shot heard around the world.
—Ralph Waldo Emerson, "Concord Hymn,"
April 19, 1837

Mid pleasures and palaces though we may roam,
Be it ever so humble, there's no place like home.
—John Howard Payne, "Home, Sweet Home,"
from the opera *Clari, the Maid of Milan,* 1823

Then conquer we must, for our cause it is just . . .
—Francis Scott Key, "The Star Spangled Banner,"
September 14, 1814

Or this bit of folklore:

I eat my peas with honey,
I've done so all my life,
It makes the peas taste funny
But it keeps them on my knife—

Or the oft-repeated lines of Dorothy Parker

Men never make passes
At girls who wear glasses.

You need not limit rhyme to song, or even poetry—good
or bad. It makes any statement noticeable, memorable, and
quotable.

Man proposes, but God disposes.
—Thomas à Kempis (1380–1471)

Genius is one percent inspiration and ninety-nine percent perspiration.

—Thomas Edison

And the paraphrase of James Otis's remarks before the Superior Court of Massachusetts in 1761:

Taxation without representation is tyranny.

Adlai Stevenson's comment, oft repeated, from his speech accepting the Democratic nomination for president, July 26, 1952:

. . . there are no gains without pains.

Rhyme can be carried further to make a message noticed. Thus Winston Churchill's message to President Franklin D. Roosevelt on the eve of the 1945 conference:

No more let us falter! From Malta to Yalta! Let nobody alter!

And later, the ultimate rhyme:

The record of the Labour Government is—Abadan, Sudan, Bevan.

And his description of life as a diplomat:

Protocol, Geritol and alcohol.

Aristocracy was described by Margot Asquith as:

Rectitude, platitude, high-hatitude.

And an epitaph for John Camden Hotten:

Hotten
Rotten
Forgotten

Robert Browning noted of love:

How sad and bad and mad it was! But then, how it was sweet!

Rhyme is everywhere, with almost unlimited utility. In politics Adlai Stevenson is credited with:

If you would make a speech or write one
Or get an artist to indite one,
Think not because 'tis understood
By men of sense, 'tis therefore good
Make it so clear and simply planned
No blockhead can misunderstand.

Memorable too are these rhymes of many occasions:

The hostess with the mostest on the ball . . .
                    —Irving Berlin, from *Call Me Madam*

We've studied the map and found to our horror, there's no such place as Glocca Morra!
                    —*The Wall Street Journal*

There's no experience less rewarding than saying thanks to a voice recording.
                    —Suzanne Douglas, *Good Housekeeping*

As a rule man is a fool,
When it's hot he wants it cool,
When it's cool he wants it hot,
Always wanting what is not.

What men call gallantry, and
    gods adultery,
Is much more common
    where the climate's sultry.
                    —George Gordon Lord Byron

There was an old woman who lived in a shoe. She didn't
    have any children—
She knew what to do.
                    —*V. F. W. Magazine*

Ogden Nash has given us many classics. One is:

Candy is dandy but liquor is quicker.

Even mock rhyme can be effective—and of course, funny:

Whenever I behold an asp
I can't suppress a prudish gasp
I do not charge the asp with matricide
But what about his cleopatricide?

The pious ones of Plymouth, reaching the Rock, first fell upon their knees, and then upon the Aborigines.

—William Evarts

Miss Teyte, a leading soprano with the Boston Opera Company, found this line of graffiti scrawled on her dressing-room mirror with lipstick one day in 1889:

Twinkle, twinkle, little star,
Who the hell do you think you are?

And a contemporary bit reads:

The doctors cure all kinds of ills
Except the shock of doctor's bills.

Jingle slogans are widely and effectively used devices utilizing rhyme. From American history we can recall:

Tippecanoe and Tyler too!

Van, Van is a used up man.

Keep cool with Coolidge.

All the way with Adlai.

And not so long ago:

Better red than dead.

The family that prays together stays together.

There are memorable advertising slogans too:

Winston tastes good like a cigarette should.

The knit that fits while she sits.

Parody of rhyme is an intriguing challenge:

> **What Hiawatha Probably Did**
> He slew the noble Mudjekeewis,
> With his skin he made him mittens;
> Made them with the fur side inside;
> Made them with the skin-side outside;
> He, to keep the warm side inside,
> Put the cold side, skin-side outside;
> He, to keep the cold side outside,
> Put the warm side, fur-side, inside:—
> That's why he put the cold side outside,
> Why he put the warm side inside,
> Why he turned them inside outside.
>
> —Anonymous

Rhyme has many rhetorical cousins, less obvious, but often more subtly effective.

ASSONANCE

Assonance, from the Latin "to sound to," involves the use of similar vowel sounds with differing consonant sounds between them or close by. A common example is:

> We do not quite forgive a giver. The hand that feeds us is in some danger of being bitten.
>
> —Ralph Waldo Emerson

> There are gatherers and scatterers of work. You, Edna, are a gatherer.
>
> —Condé Nast, of Edna Woolman Chase

> In statesmanship, get the formalities right, never mind the moralities.
>
> —Mark Twain

> His poetry alternates between the appealing and the appalling.

When the endings sound alike the term *simile determina-*

tione (Latin for alike in ending), or *homoioteleuton* (Greek for "like ending") applies:

> May we know unity without conformity.
> —Dwight D. Eisenhower

> Life is a struggle to keep earning capacity to yearning capacity.

> Natural man has only two primal passions: to get and to beget.
> —Sir William Osler

> The best ability you have is reliability.
> —Elmer G. Letterman

> The worst buy is an alibi.

> The ballot is stronger than the bullet.
> —Abraham Lincoln

> Politics is the career of plundering and blundering.
> —Disraeli

By placing parallel sounds in equal clauses you get a kind of assonance that the Greeks called *paronomasis*, meaning "to pun with similar but not identical sounds," of which more will be said later. This usually involves the change of a single letter. The Romans called it *agnominatio* meaning "two words of different meaning but similar sound brought together."

> I would live all my life in nonchalance and insouciance were it not for making a living, which is rather a nouciance.
> —Ogden Nash

More seriously:

> The most incomprehensible thing about the world is that it is comprehensible.
> —Albert Einstein

Some of us throw bombs. I throw ideas. We have men to do the shooting, but I do the shouting.
—M'hammed Yazid, for rebel Algeria, 1961

We are now facing a problem more of ethics than physics.
—Bernard M. Baruch

What we need today is not a reformulation of national purpose but a recollection of national purpose.
—*Saturday Review*

Just as assonance is a figurative cousin to rhyme, consonance is a cousin to alliteration. To achieve consonance you use similar (but not identical) stressed consonant sounds with differing vowels and differing stress.

Gaunt as the ghastliest of glimpses that gleam
through the gloom of the gloaming when ghosts go aghast
—Algernon Charles Swinburne, "Nephelidia"

'Twas sooner when the cricket went
Than when the winter came
Yet that pathetic pendulum
Keeps esoteric time.
—Emily Dickinson

However, you must use these devices with care. It is generally considered "unacceptable" to place in juxtaposition similar sounds without a meaningful pattern. Even rhyme within a sentence, when not related to a rhythm, can be jarring. Witness: "The wind destroyed a fine pine clinging to the blind valley." Or: "He gave consideration to Tom's interpretation of the industrial Revolution."

On the other hand, you can use this dis-euphony effectively as a "stopper" to make a sentence stand out from the page. "An allegation of integration was the motivation for the conflagration."

ALLITERATION

Alliteration is another obvious, easily applied, and widely utilized device. It originally involved a recurrence of initial sounds, a form of consonance, but today generally includes vowels, i.e., assonance. Its ultimate is the Greek *parimion*, meaning "closely resembling," where every word in a sentence, phrase, or expression begins with the same letter.

Thus the widely quoted:

Peter Piper picked a peck of pickled peppers.

which one advertiser adapted:

Peter Piper picked a pair of Pendleton plaids from Portland.

And:

Powerful people aren't impressed by paper tigers.
   —*San Francisco Chronicle-San Francisco Examiner*

That was the Week that Was.
   —Title of the 1962 BBC show

Its members are quite hopeless—drooling, driveling, doleful, depressing, dropsical drips.
   —Sir Thomas Beecham

Penitence must precede pardon.
   —John Adams

Pencil, pad and purpose.
   —Edna Ferber, of Edmund Wilson

Screaming, sooty, scythe-winged, short-tailed sprite that makes a swallow seem slow.
   —James Fisher

And the Bible has its share:

Her ways are ways of pleasantness, and all her paths are peace.
—Proverbs 3:17

For most writings, you can use simple alliteration to create attention:

Peace is our passion.
—Thomas Jefferson

The dreadful dead of dark midnight.
—William Shakespeare, "The Rape of Lucrece"

A pinch of probably is worth a pound of perhaps.
—James Thurber, *Lanterns and Lances*

Your alliteration need not be so consistent:

What we lawyers want to do is to substitute courts for carnage, dockets for rockets, briefs for bombs, warrants for warheads, mandates for missiles . . .
—Charles Rhyne, Chairman, World Conference on World Peace Through Law

You can also take alliteration to the absurd with the tongue twister:

A tooter who tooted a flute
  Tried to tutor two tutors to toot.
Said the two to the tutor,
  "Is it harder to toot or
To tutor two tutors to toot?"

I never felt felt that felt
like that felt felt.

The bear could not bear the boar,
  The boar thought the bear a bore.
At last the bear could bear no more
  That boar that bored him on the moor,
And so one morn he bored the boar—
That boar will bore the bear no more.

If one doctor doctors another, does the doctor who doctors the doctor doctor the doctor the way the doctor he is doctoring doctors? Or does he doctor the doctor the way the doctor doctors doctors?

I never smelled a smelt that smelled as bad as that smelt smelled.

ONOMATOPOEIA

Onomatopoeia, despite its wide contemporary usage, was first conceived by the Greeks. The term translates as "the making of words." It is currently defined as the invention of words that sound like their meaning. Roman rhetoricians have variously called it *nominatio* (meaning "naming"), *procreatio* ("breeding"), and *nominis fictio* ("feigning of a name"). Puttenham called it *newnamer.* All realized that association of the sound of a word with its meaning is basic to the origins of human language. If we were to seek the sources of words through intensive analysis, the atoms of language would probably be largely verbalized sounds suggested by the objects and actions, either directly or by analogy. By selecting words with the background sounds analogous to the image, the force of your communication achieves an additional dimension.

We can distinguish two types of onomatopoeia: that which reproduces the sound directly, and that which suggests the sound.

Classics of direct sounds, sometimes called echo writing, include such words as riffraff, dingdong, cuckoo clock, Ping-Pong, buzz.

> To the tintinnabulation that so
>   musically wells
> From the bells, bells, bells, bells,
> Bells, bells, bells—
> From the jingling and the tinkling
>   of the bells.
>   —Edgar Allan Poe

The murmur of innumerable bees.

And frowsy tinklings lull the distant folds.

—Thomas Gray

Women's Tea: giggle, gobble, gabble.

—Oliver Wendell Holmes

Renowned for his use of the sound of words was Edgar Allan Poe. This is from the onomatopoeic "The Raven":

> And the silken sad uncertain rustling
>   of each purple curtain thrilled me—
> filled me with fantastic terrors
> never felt before;
> So that now, to still the beating of my heart,
> I stood repeating;
> " 'Tis some visitor entreating entrance at my
> chamber door—
> Some late visitor entreating entrance at my
> chamber door;
>   This it is and nothing more."

For onomatopoeic suggestion we note:

The murmurous haunt of flies on summer eves.

—John Keats

Do not let us speak of darker days, let us speak rather of sterner days. These are not dark days: these are great days.

—Winston Churchill

The very name London has tonnage in it.

—V. S. Pritchett

Describing World War II, General Douglas MacArthur comments:

In my dreams I hear again the crash of guns, the rattle of musketry, the strange, mournful mutter of the battlefield.

And this is a description of the speechmaking of John L. Lewis by David Brinkley, NBC commentator:

. . . rhetoric that rolls like a freight train over a bridge.

A somnolent effect is achieved by Alfred Tennyson in the poem "The Lotus-Eaters":

How sweet it were. . . .
To lend our hearts and spirits wholly
To the music of mild-minded melancholy;
To muse and brood and live again in memory.

Here is another contemporary example:

Over and through all that I see there is woven an endless quiet—
the quiet of the sky which earth's voices never interrupt. Now
and then a goldfinch charges by, uttering his staccato warble at
each downward plunge. A nuthatch, at work in the wood below me, calls at odd intervals in his nasal contralto. A cicada,
wakened by the sun that feels like August, tears the seam of
silence furiously at every third minute. Crickets are chirping all
about, giving thanks in a hundred voices for a day entirely to
their mind.

—Odell Shepard, *Harvest of a Quiet Eye*

Sometimes a single mouth-filling word carries its own sug-
gestiveness:

bamboozles
blunderbuss
nincompoop
curmudgeon
lackadaisical
rambunctious
scalawag

SUBLIMINAL APPEALS

The appeal to the non-aural senses through the use of words
is a development of modern subliminal suggestion techniques.

It is an imaginative—and a difficult—figure to use, but advertising copywriters often try. Frequently, this involves *synesthesia,* a figure of speech in which you stimulate one sense by means of an image that would normally appeal to another sense, as in "hearing" color. In many instances you'll find euphony and onomatopoeia handy in achieving these effects.

It's like bathing your face in champagne!

—Beauty Ice

The first brandy of Spain will make love to your tastebuds.

—Fundador

You get acceleration as easy as a giant's stride, a liquid grace in motion, steering as sharp and precise as a scalpel.

—Corvette

See the sky. Hear the gulls. Smell the clean salt air. Come to your senses.

—Virginia Beach

Taste the good times

—Raleigh cigarettes

You can almost hear the sea.

—Windrift cologne

Under a picture of a passionate scene:

the french have a way without words
it's cardin de pierre cardin.

Of course the most obvious device—not unusual in advertising of every type—is the picture of a beautiful woman —with or without comment . . . or covering.

Tonight, make it with Kijafa.

Much good writing makes use of euphony in this subtle way to create the setting in sound or imagery. A noted classical example is Sir Thomas Browne's meditation when he discovered Roman burial urns at Norwich. Commenting on the way men were buried in times past, he mocks men's dreams of immortality:

> Now since these dead bones have already out-lasted the living ones of Methuselah, and in a yard under ground, and thin walls of clay, out-worn all the strong and specious building above it; and quietly rested under the drums and tramplings of three conquests; what prince can promise such diuturnity unto his relics. . . .

And again in John Masefield's "Cargoes," the words are harsh to contrast with soft words in the earlier stanzas:

> With a cargo of Tyne coal,
> Road-rails, pig-lead,
> Fire-wood, iron-ware and cheap tin trays.

Lewis Carroll made sensual nonsense poetry famous with "Jabberwocky" in *Alice*. These lines are more than nice noises:

> 'Twas brillig, and the slithy toves
> Did gyre and gimble in the wabe:
> All mimsy were the borogoves,
> And the mome raths outgrabe.

Gertrude Stein carried the concept to a new dimension with a technique of reiteration, a sort of melody of words.

> a Petticoat
> A light, white, a disgrace, an ink spot, a rosy charm.

The philosophy of Stein's writing assumed that people grew to love what they repeated, and what they repeated they loved:

> Sweet sweet sweet sweet sweet tea.
> Susie Asado.
> Sweet sweet sweet sweet sweet tea
> Susie Asado
> Susie Asado which is a told tray sure.

VISUAL DEVICES

In a literary world, you can still use an appeal to the visual senses, to attract attention or to make a point, or to facilitate memory. The paragraph, the indented line in poetry, are thus effective for ordinary usage. Prayer books make much use of the acrostic.

Juvenile literature and sales letters have in common the use of the shaped message.

It is Hard

To forget
 apologize
 save money
 be unselfish
 avoid mistakes
 keep out of a rut
 begin all over again
 make the best of all things
 keep your temper all the time
 think before you act
 maintain a high standard
 keep on keeping on
 shoulder blame
 be charitable
But it pays to
 admit error
 take advice
 forgive

ON THE STREET

He bought a little block of stock
The day he went to town;
And in the nature of such things,
  That
  Stock
  Went
  Right
  Straight
  Down!

He sold a little block of stock:
Now sorrow fills his cup,
For from the moment that he did,
Up.
Right
Went
Thing
Blamed
The

He bought a little block of stock,
Expecting he would taste of bliss;
He can't let go and can't hang on,

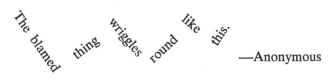

—Anonymous

Ladder placement of ideas seems unsophisticated but it carries a message effectively:

	Ladder of success
100%	I did
90%	I will
80%	I can
70%	I think I can
60%	I might
50%	I think I might
40%	What is it
30%	I wish I could
20%	I don't know how
10%	I can't
0%	I won't

Soldier's shoulders h d d e
                    s u   r

when S H R I L L
shells *S H R I E K*.

The
sinking
steamer
sunk

L st & Found
—Clyde Beilla

The rush-hour traffic I'd just as soon miss
When caraftercarismovinglikethis.
—Robert Lawler

A more sophisticated approach is found by Allen Ginsberg

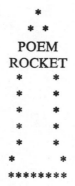

POEM
ROCKET

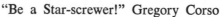

"Be a Star-screwer!" Gregory Corso

Or utilizing the format of a recipe:

Recipe for Happiness
1 cup filled with
Industry
Concentration
Enthusiasm
1 pinch of spice
1 pinch of sand
Served with sauce of smiles.

Every organization has four kinds of workers
Jaw-bone
Wish-bone
Back-bone
Knee-bone

I blesse thee, Lord, because I GROW
Among thy trees, which in a ROW
To thee both fruit and order OWE.
What open force, or hidden CHARM
Can blast my fruit, or bring me HARM.
While the inclosure is thine ARM?
Inclose me still for fear I START.
Be to me rather sharp and TART,
Then let me want thy hand & ART.
When thou dost greater judgments SPARE,
And with thy knife but prune and PARE,
Ev'n fruitfull trees more fruitfull ARE.

Even in the sixteenth century Henry Peacham described formations as lozenges, pillars, quadrangles, and other shapes in typesetting.

A contemporary use is:

Wendy
Watts
Leans
On
Klopman
Fabrics

or

If your direct mail messages
fall *FLAT*. . .

or

Take the easy way up* Air Canada

ETC.

The rebus, widely used in contest puzzles, also has a place in communication. *Webster's Third* repeats a classic in its definition: ICURYY4me (I see you are too wise for me). Others:

> This means U!
>
> Ch U rch
>
> cens U S
>
> Our church needs U to help.
>
> We are counting on U.
> > —*The Sunday School Builder*

Advertisers pun in this way:

UNITED . . . even our name begins with YOU.
> —United Van Lines

Union Dime Savings Bank—the dime that starts with "U."

CHAPTER

V

SCHEMES—FIGURES
OF STRUCTURE

OUR ORATOR ANCESTORS CONSIDERED THE FORMATION OF patterned sentences as the "easy figures" of rhetoric. The difficult figures involved imagery—metaphor, simile, hyperbole, synecdoche, etc. Although these "easy figures" are widely used in writing today—particularly persuasive writing—most of us use them automatically, with little thought to the patterns involved. In fact, most fine writers or public speakers develop so distinctive a pattern or style that a quotation may often be identified even out of context. This style may involve such elements as sentence structure, rhythm, or a distinctive use of vocabulary. The styles of Roosevelt, Kennedy, Stevenson, each had a personality of its own, utilizing devices taught and learned by a hundred generations of scholars as figures of speech, structure, thought, and diction. The great writings of the Western world are filled with them.

The "scheme" in rhetoric is a pattern of words that does not affect the literal sense of the words. Some rhetoricians consider these to be the true figures of speech, but in any case, they are distinct from the group known as trope, in which the meaning or significance of the words changes. Most of these schemes were described long ago by Aristotle, Cicero, and others, but a few have evolved in modern times.

BALANCE

You may achieve balance in a communication in various ways, but the most usual method is through the use of similar or identical structures:

> The seeds ye sow—another reaps,
> The robes ye weave—another wears,
> The arms ye forge—another bears.
> —Percy Bysshe Shelley

We hold these truths to be self-evident: that all men are created equal; that they . . .
> —Thomas Jefferson

United we stand, divided we fall.
> —Motto of the State of Kentucky, 1792

An advertiser uses balance thus:

The Arabs invented it. The French found a word for it. The New School has a class in it.

All of the easy figures, the schemes, result in balance of a sort.

EQUAL LENGTH

The simplest scheme, and one of the first to be used, is the *isocolon,* widely used in oratory. Here you repeat phrases of equal length and, usually, of similar structure. The term comes from the Greek "of equal members or clauses," and related to it are *compar, parison, parimembre,* and Puttenham's term, *even.* All of these involve balancing clauses of equal lengths. Thus William Shakespeare, in *Love's Labours Lost*:

> Your reasons at dinner have
> been sharp and sententious;

> pleasant without scurrility,
> witty without affectation, audacious
> without impudency, learned
> without opinion, and strange
> without heresy.

In the *Book of Common Prayer,* we find:

> Earth to earth, ashes to ashes, dust to dust, in sure and certain
> hope of the resurrection.

In the Bible:

> Eye for eye, tooth for tooth, hand for hand, foot for foot.
> —Deuteronomy, 19:21

> We come and we cry, and this is life; we yawn and we depart,
> and this is death!
> —Ausone de Chancel

> Geography has made us neighbors. History has made us friends.
> Economics has made us partners; and necessity has made us
> allies.
> —John F. Kennedy

> Indomitable in retreat; invincible in advance; insufferable in
> victory!
> —Winston Churchill of Charles de Gaulle

> Follow me if I advance! Kill me if I retreat! Revenge me if I die!
> —Ngo Dinh Diem

> Men will wrangle for religion; write for it; fight for it; die for it;
> anything but live it.
> —Walter Colton

> Laws too gentle are seldom obeyed; too severe, seldom exe-
> cuted.
> —Benjamin Franklin

DOUBLING

The same word repeated was termed *epizeuxis* by the Greeks, meaning "fastening upon." Romans called it *geminatio,* meaning "doubling." Puttenham called it *cuckowspell* or *underlay.* The purpose is usually for emphasis. You can achieve a powerful effect by repeating only one word:

The Yanks! The Yanks!

Patience. Patience. Patience! The first, the last, the middle virtue of a politician.

—John Adams

. . . a man of charm, charm, charm and luck, luck, luck.

—Leonard Mosley, of Lord Mountbatten

Nonsense, simply nonsense . . .

—Walt Whitman

Backward, turn backward, O Time, in your flight,
Make me a child again, just for tonight.

—Elizabeth Chase Akers

Break, break, break,
On thy cold gray stones, O sea!
And I would that my tongue could utter
The thoughts that arise in me

—Alfred Tennyson

Alone, alone, all, all alone,
Alone on a wide, wide sea.

—Samuel Taylor Coleridge

If I were an American, as I am an Englishman, while a foreign troop was landed in my country I never would lay down my arms,—never! never! never!

—William Pitt

Doubling is often used in radio and television advertising to impress the name of a product:

It's delicious champagne. It's delicious Martini and Rossi Asti Spumanti.

You can create an equally compelling effect by repeating a word or phrase, even with a word or a few words in between. Of these, probably the most quoted is Franklin D. Roosevelt's:

. . . the only thing we have to fear is fear itself.

There are also well-known expressions, such as:

I believe in the greatest good to the greatest number.
—Ulysses S. Grant

Vanity of vanities; all is vanity.
—Ecclesiastes 1:2

Let our object be our country, our whole country, and nothing but our country. And, by the blessing of God, may that country itself become a vast and splendid monument, not of oppression and terror, but of wisdom, of peace and of liberty, upon which the world may gaze with admiration forever.
—Daniel Webster

Citizenship is man's basic right, for it is nothing less than the right to have rights.
—Earl Warren

The government is us, we are the government, you and I.
—Theodore Roosevelt, 1902

O, it's a snug little island!
A right little, tight little island!
—Thomas Dibdin

One flag, one land, one heart,
One hand, one nation evermore.

My creed is this:
Happiness is the only good.
The place to be happy is here.
The time to be happy is now.
The way to be happy is to help make others so.
                              —Robert Green Ingersoll

It has been said that the only thing we learn from history is
that we do not learn.
                    —Chief Justice Earl Warren, in a eulogy for
                    John F. Kennedy

All the ills of democracy can be cured by more democracy.
                              —Alfred E. Smith

Only Americans can hurt America.
                              —Dwight D. Eisenhower

I got my exercise by being a pall-bearer to my friends who
exercise.
                              —Chauncey Depew

The human race has improved everything except the human
race.
                              —Adlai Stevenson

She dresses on the theory that nothing succeeds like nothing.

Advertisers use the device in this way:

Why the world's biggest truck doesn't need the world's biggest
driver.
                              —Sperry

Nearly everything they can do, we can do smaller.
                              —Pearlcorder-SR 501

Never buy a Bordeaux by the bottle
Buy a velvety Bordeaux by the label.
                              —B. & G.

Manufacturers with difficult-to-pronounce names make much use of this device in TV commercials, correcting the unsophisticated by repeating the name again and again, e.g., Fazi-Battaglia Verdicchio.

For heightening emotional impact in any statement you can use similar repetition in succeeding clauses or sentences. The Latin term is *conduplicato* meaning "repetition." Although this works well in building to a strong assertion, it seems to be used most often for negative statements. Thus, for heightened emotional effect:

> We are afraid of truth, afraid of fortune, afraid of death, and afraid of each other.
> —Ralph Waldo Emerson

> Every day was Sunday
> and every month was May
> and every girl who came along
> was sure to come your way.
> —Rod McKuen

> Ring out old shapes of foul disease
> Ring out the narrowing lust of gold
> Ring out the thousand wars of old
> Ring out the thousand years of peace.
> —Alfred Tennyson

> No pain, no palm; no thorns, no throne;
> no gall, no glory; no cross, no crown.
> —William Penn

I am in earnest—I will not equivocate—I will not excuse—I will not retreat a single inch and I will be heard.
> —William Lloyd Garrison

I had hoped it would be the conscience of the world and it is. I had hoped it would help erase the racial barriers and it has . . .
> —General Carlos P. Romulo, of the UN

Responding to the claims of General Henri Pétain after Dunkirk that "in three weeks England will have her neck wrung like a chicken," Winston Churchill proclaimed:

We have not journeyed all this way across the centuries, across the oceans, across the mountains, across the prairies, because we are made of sugar candy. . . . Some chicken; some neck.

Never in the field of human conflict was so much owed by so many to so few.
—Winston Churchill of the Royal Air Force, 1941

You can use this same technique of repetition for amplification. Instead of making a single statement, you build on additional details, examples, or reasons in order to create a more powerful conclusion.

Valor is self-respecting. Valor is circumspect. Valor strikes only when it is right to strike.
—Woodrow Wilson

Very few EDP people perform, in part because they are arrogant, in part because they are ignorant, and in part because they are too enamored of their goddamned tool.
—Peter Drucker

There are not enough jails, not enough policemen, not enough courts to enforce a law not supported by the people.
—Hubert H. Humphrey

We have not, we do not, and we will not condone, excuse, or explain away wrong-doing or moral obliquity in public office, whoever the guilty and whatever their station. . . . One corrupt official is one too many.
—Adlai Stevenson

My view is, without deviation, without exception, without any ifs, buts, or whereases, that freedom of speech means that you shall not do something to people either for the views they have, or the views they express, or the words they speak or write.

—Hugo L. Black

We will neglect our cities to our peril, for in neglecting them we neglect the nation.

—John F. Kennedy

Still another technique for giving your words power is a refrain that repeats the point at issue. This was *epimone* to the Greeks, which translates as "tarrying." The Romans called it *perseverentia,* meaning "constancy."

Refuse to be ill. Never tell people you are ill; never own it to yourself. Illness is one of those things which a man should resist on principle at the onset.

—Edward Bulwer-Lytton

We need help, and we need it yesterday.

—Mayor Carl B. Stokes

Men of different ancestries, men of different tongues, men of different colors, men of different environments, men of different geographies do not see everything alike. Even in our own country we do not see everything alike.

—Lyndon B. Johnson

Of that there is no manner of doubt—
No probable, possible shadow of doubt—
No possible doubt whatever.

—W. S. Gilbert, *The Gondoliers*

I was born an American; I live an American; I shall die as an American; and I intend to perform the duties incumbent upon me in that character to the end of my career.

—Daniel Webster

This old anonymous tirade against women is another example:

>Oh, the shrewdness of their
>shrewdness when they're
>shrewd.
>And the rudeness of their
>rudeness when they're
>rude;
>But the shrewdness of their
>shrewdness and the rude-
>ness of their rudeness,
>Are nothing to their goodness
>when they're good.

Many remember from the old-fashioned school:

>Do all the good you can,
>By all the means you can,
>In all the ways you can,
>In all the places you can,
>At all the times you can,
>To all the people you can,
>As long as ever you can.
>
>—John Wesley

For an effective use of repetition, you should consider which parts of speech you reiterate (nouns? verbs? adjectives?) and where you place the repeated words: at the beginning, in the middle, or at the end of a phrase or sentence. Careful placement of a repeated word or phrase gives a certain emphasis to an idea.

AT THE BEGINNING

One of the most powerful techniques is to repeat a word or phrase at the beginning of a series of clauses. This was called *anaphora* ("carrying back") or *epembasis* ("advance") by the Greeks, *repetitio* or *iteratio* ("repetition") by the Romans, and *report* by Puttenham. There are a variety of approaches, but none of the following would be as effective if the repetition did not come at the beginning. Note that in all of these examples the words or phrase that are repeated become less important than the words that follow, and that in many of them, the writer begins with the least important idea and leads up to the most important at the end of the quotation.

. . . first in war, first in peace, first in the hearts of his countrymen.
> —Henry ("Light Horse Harry") Lee, in Congress, five days after Washington's death

When everyone is in the wrong, everyone is in the right.
> —Francois d'Arx de La Chaussée

Money talks, money prints: money broadcasts: money reigns, and kings and labor leaders alike have to register its decrees, and even, by a staggering paradox, to finance its enterprises and guarantee its profits. Democracy is no longer bought; it is bilked.
> —George Bernard Shaw

I am fighting, as I have always fought, for the rights of the little man as well as for the big man—for the weak as well as for the strong . . . I am fighting to keep this nation prosperous and at peace. I am fighting to keep our people out of foreign wars, and to keep foreign conceptions of government out of our own United States. I am fighting for these great and good causes. I am fighting to defend them against the power and might of those who rise up to challenge them. And I will not stop fighting.
> —Franklin D. Roosevelt

It is in the soil of ignorance that poverty is planted. It is in the soil of ignorance that disease flourishes. It is in the soil of ignorance that racial and religious strife takes root. It is in the soil of ignorance that Communism brings forth the bitter fruit of tyranny.

—Lyndon B. Johnson

Give up money, give up fame, give up science, give up the earth itself and all it contains, rather than do an immoral act.

—Thomas Jefferson

Peace is art. Peace is when time doesn't matter as it passes by.

—Maria Schell

Civil wrongs don't make civil rights . . . civil wrongs probably only beget civil wrongs.

—Adlai Stevenson

. . . knowledge is power . . . knowledge is safety, and . . . knowledge is happiness.

—Thomas Jefferson

A contemporary use in advertising is presented by McGraw-Hill Magazines:

> I don't know who you are.
> I don't know your company.
> I don't know your company's product.
> I don't know what your company stands for.
> I don't know your company's customers.
> I don't know your company's record.
> I don't know your company's reputation.
> Now—what was it you wanted to sell me?

> Grand new looks.
> Grand new luxury.
> Grand new Prix.

—Pontiac

More simply applied:

The more you perspire, the more you need Mitchum.

> Very pretty.
> Very feminine.
> Very, very exciting.
>
> —Cerissa by Charles Revson

Or Amtrak's:

> Lots of trains.
> Lots of places.
> Not a lot of money.

This device can also serve as onomatopoeia:

> What has my life been? Fag and grind, fag and grind. Turn the wheel, turn the wheel.
>
> —Charles Dickens

or elicit an emotional response:

> Those evening bells! Those evening bells!

or be used for simple emphasis:

> I am attached to you. But I can't consent and won't consent and I never did consent and I never will consent to be lost in you.
>
> —Charles Dickens

Here is a well-remembered paragraph that involves several schemes:

> The vision of America will never change. America once, when she was a little people, sat upon a hill of privilege and had a vision of the future. She saw men happy because they were free. She saw them free because they were equal. She saw them banded together because they had the spirit of brothers. She saw them safe because they did not wish to impose upon one another. And the vision is not changed. The multitude has grown, that welcome multitude that comes from all parts of the world to seek a safe place of life and hope in America. And so America will move forward, if she moves forward at all, only with her face to that same sun of promise.
>
> —Woodrow Wilson

SIDE BY SIDE

To achieve a more balanced emphasis than you get by placing your repetition at the beginning of a clause or phrase, you can use the device called *parataxis* by the Greeks. This device, translated as "placing side by side," means that you arrange your independent phrases or clauses as coordinates, that is, parts with equal grammatical weight, rather than use subordinate clauses and phrases. The effect is to give the same importance to each component of your sentence or paragraph.

I came, I saw, I conquered.

—Julius Caesar

Men are four:
He who knows not and knows not he knows not,
  he is a fool—shun him;
He who knows not and knows he knows not,
  he is simple—teach him;
He who knows and knows not he knows,
  he is asleep—wake him;
He who knows and knows he knows,
  he is wise—follow him!

—Arabic apothegm

AT THE END

Repetition of a word or phrase at the end of a series of clauses was what the Greeks called *antistrophe,* meaning "turning about," or *epistrophe,* meaning "turning away," or *epiphora,* meaning "a bringing upon." The Romans called it *conversio* ("turning around"), and Puttenham called it *counterturne.* This kind of repetition serves to emphasize the repeated word or phrase, since it is the last thing your audience will hear and so sticks in their minds.

A democracy, that is, a government of all the people, by all the people, for all the people . . .

> —Rev. Theodore Parker

The government was created by the States, is amenable to the States, is preserved by the States, and may be destroyed by the States . . . I owe no responsibility, politically speaking, elsewhere than to my State. . . .

> —John Tyler

To avoid criticism, say nothing, do nothing, be nothing.

Some men are born great, some achieve greatness, and some have greatness thrust upon them.

> —William Shakespeare

This passage from Corinthians 13:11 is given by Henry Peacham as an example:

When I was a child, I spake as a child, I understood as a child, I thought as a child: but when I became a man, I put away childish things.

LIKE ENDINGS

Homoioteleuton—the Greek meaning "like ending"—refers to a series of elements that conclude alike—a variation of rhyme as we know it. Some variations include putting the similar grammatical cases or phrases at the end of the clauses or sentences, at the beginning or the middle, or in the middle of one clause and the beginning of another.

Put up or shut up.

> —Eighteenth century expression used in early
> stock markets, and later at gaming tables

To get along, go along.

> —Sam Rayburn's advice to new members
> of Congress, 1950s

Our opinions agree as to the evil, moral, political, and economical, of slavery.

—James Madison

The first wealth is health.

—Ralph Waldo Emerson, 1850

He serves his party best who serves his country best.

—Rutherford B. Hayes, 1877

We learn nothing from history except that we learn nothing from history.

—Heinrich Heine

This adaptation was made for a recent advertisement (including the pun):

If I don't want you to go right by me, I've got to do right by you.

The runaway leader in business jets is on the runway.

—*Canadian Challenger*

AND IN BETWEEN

Repetition of a word at the end of one clause and the beginning of the next was called *anadiplosis* (translated "doubling back") by the Greeks and *duplicatio* by the Romans. Puttenham called it *redouble*. It is usually used with nouns in apposition.

We stand today on the edge of a new frontier, a frontier of unknown opportunities and perils, a frontier of unfulfilled hopes and threats.

—John F. Kennedy

Our ultimate good is a world without war, a world made safe for diversity, in which all men, goods and ideas can freely move across every border and every boundary.

—Lyndon B. Johnson

The device can be used in cases other than apposition:

Never trouble trouble till trouble troubles you.
—Benjamin Franklin

THE FRAME

You may also repeat a word or phrase at the beginning of each of a series of expressions and another word at the end of each of the series, like a frame. This was called *symploce* by the Greeks, translated as "intertwining." The Romans called it *comprehension* which translates as "seizing with the hands," or *completio* meaning "combination." Puttenham's term was *replie*.

I was born in England, I will fight for England and die in England. But I'm damned if I'll live in England."
—Sir Cedric Hardwicke

Poor doll's dressmaker! How often so dragged down by hands that should have raised her up; how often so misdirected when losing her way on the eternal road and asking guidance. Poor little doll's dressmaker.
—Charles Dickens

Repetition of words in inverted order—the Greeks called it *antimetabole* (meaning "turning about"), the Romans *commutatio* (meaning "interchange"), Puttenham called it *counterchange*—is another device.

There are those who hate love and love hate.

In him was vindicated the greatness of real goodness and the goodness of real greatness.
—Rev. Phillips Brooks of Abraham Lincoln

Let us never negotiate out of fear. But let us never fear to negotiate.
—John F. Kennedy

We cannot always build the future for our youth, but we can build our youth for the future.

—Franklin D. Roosevelt

Man is not the creature of circumstances; circumstances are the creatures of men.

—Benjamin Disraeli

If a man owns land, the land owns him.

—Ralph Waldo Emerson

Trifles make perfection, and perfection is no trifle.

—Michelangelo

Learn to live, and live to learn.

—Bayard Taylor

I would rather forget to drink than drink to forget.

—Temperance slogan at the turn of the century

The device can be used with less directness:

A government that is big enough to give you all you want is big enough to take it all away.

—Barry M. Goldwater

Happiness doesn't come from doing what we like to do but from liking what we have to do.

—Wilfred Peterson

Somebody loses whenever somebody wins.

—Carl Sandburg

. . . nobody will care for him who cares for nobody.

—Thomas Jefferson

There is no remedy for love but to love more.

—Henry David Thoreau

Whatever America hopes to bring to pass in the world must first come to pass in the heart of America.

—Dwight D. Eisenhower

Where there's marriage without love, there will be love without marriage.

—Benjamin Franklin

Business Week uses the device in this way:

Do your executives know more and more about less and less?

The use is not uncommon in literature:

. . . men's happiness depends upon their expectations—and the expectations of modern men have grown tremendously.

—Charles Frankel, *The Case for Modern Man*, 1956

All happy families are alike, but each unhappy family is unhappy in its own way.

—Tolstoy, *Anna Karenina*

. . . the world is hard to love, though we must love it because we have no other, and to fail to love it is not to exist at all.

—Mark Van Doren

Writers seldom write the things they think. They simply write the things they think other folks think they think.

—Elbert Hubbard

SAME WORD, DIFFERENT SENSE

The repetition of a word with a new sense was called by the Greeks *ploce* (meaning "plaiting"), and the Romans, *traductio* (meaning "leading along") or *copulatio* (meaning "joining"). Puttenham called it *swift repeate*. The most common use is the expression: "Thank you, but no thank you."

We must indeed all hang together, or, most assuredly, we shall all hang separately.

> —Benjamin Franklin, at the signing
> of the Declaration of Independence

When the going gets tough, the tough get going.

"We have been talking and talking about the difficulties of growth," a ranking Communist official said of the party. "Now we have come to the growth of difficulties."

> —*The New York Times,* 1976

This headline from a recent advertisement makes use of the device:

Why doesn't anyone tell you there's a difference between making love and being in love?

Here are some others:

It's not just good for you. It's good.

> —Bran Chex

Bet with your head, not over it.

> —OTB

You may also repeat a word with the same root but a different ending. This was called in Greek *polyptoton* and in Latin *adnominatio* ("two words of different meaning but with similar source brought together").

May we pursue the right without self-righteousness.

> —Dwight D. Eisenhower

All mankind love a lover.

> —Ralph Waldo Emerson

Common sense is very uncommon.

Next to ingratitude, the most painful thing to bear is gratitude.
> —Rev. Henry Ward Beecher

A gentleman is a man who can disagree without being disagreeable.

A cult of culture has risen from the general increase in wealth, leisure and education.

—Eric Sevareid

Bear and forbear.

—Epictetus

I never found the companion that was so companionable as solitude.

—Henry David Thoreau

It is also used by advertisers:

There are some workers Workers' Compensation doesn't compensate.

—Utica National Insurance Group

Sometimes these kinds of repetitions are called *traductio*, Latin for "leading along." Puttenham called this *translacer*. Here the device is used with the same prefix:

A committee is a group of the unfit, appointed by the unwilling to do the unnecessary.

—Victor Riesel

I see one-third of a nation ill-housed, ill-clad, ill-nourished.

—Franklin D. Roosevelt, 1937

What the candidate must get across is that he is unslick, unrich, unprofessional, unestablishment.

—William Greidet

In an advertisement:

New York to L.A. Non-stop. Non-cramped.

Here is a variation, using colloquialisms that all have the same ending:

Three democrats lead for president, Adlai Stevenson, Stuart Symington and Jack Kennedy—the egghead, warhead and mophead.

—Fletcher Knebel

This device can be adapted for a humorous effect:

Husbands come in three grades: prizes, surprises and consolation prizes.

Here is a use in contemporary advertising:

Get an earful from a handful with Olympus.

—Portable tape recorders

A more definitive change in meaning is noted by the Greek term *antistasis*, translated "opposition," in which you use the same word in a different or contrary sense. The Romans called this *contentio*, meaning "despite."

The business of America is business.

—Calvin Coolidge, 1925

The place to stop crime is in the high chair, not in the electric chair.

—Jonah Goldstein

Put not your trust in money, but put your money in trust.

—Oliver Wendell Holmes

It appears in an advertisement:

When business brings you to South Texas, bring your business to us.

—Cullen/Frost Bankers, Inc.

Another device that can incorporate repetition, usually to achieve a certain poetic rhythm, is *effectio*, from the Latin "fashion." This is a personal description, sometimes as head-to-toe listing, as in "The Village Blacksmith" by Longfellow:

> The smith, a mighty man is he
> With large and sinewy hands; . . .

His hair is crisp, and black, and long,
His face is like the tan;
His brow is wet with honest sweat . . .

or this from Bartholomew Griffin's *Fidessa*:

My Lady's hair is threads of beaten gold,
Her front the purest Chrystal eye hath seen:
Her eyes the brightest stars the heavens hold,
Her cheeks red roses such as seld have been:
Her pretty lips of red vermillion dye,
Her hands of ivory the purest white:
Her blush Aurora, or the morning sky,
Her breast displays two silver fountains bright,
The Spheres her voice, her grace the Graces three,
Her body is the Saint that I adore,
Her smiles and favors sweet as honey be,
Her feet fair Thetis praiseth evermore.
But ah the worst and last is yet behind,
For of a Gryphon she doth bear the mind.

DWELLING UPON

Another way to emphasize a strong point is to repeat it a number of times in different words. The Romans called this method *commoratio*, meaning "dwelling"; Puttenham called it *abode*.

I never engaged in public affairs for my own interest, pleasure, envy, jealousy, avarice or ambition, or even the desire of fame.
—John Adams

With malice toward none; with charity for all; with firmness in the right, as God gives us to see the right . . .
—Abraham Lincoln

It is, Sir, the people's Constitution, the people's government, made for the people, made by the people, and answerable to the people.
—Daniel Webster

We shall fight on the beaches, we shall fight on the landing grounds, we shall fight in the fields and in the streets, we shall fight in the hills; we shall never surrender. And [in an aside to a colleague, as the House thundered with cheers] . . . we will fight them with the butt end of broken bottles because that's bloody well all we've got."

—Winston Churchill, 1940

When two people are under the influence of the most violent, most insane, most delusive, and most transient of passions, they are required to swear that they will remain in the excited, abnormal, and exhausting condition continuously until death do them part.

—George Bernard Shaw, *Getting Married*

WORKING OUT

Still another way to gain emphasis through repetition is with a device called *exergasia* ("working out") in Greek and *expolitio* ("polishing" or "embellishing") in Latin. It is essentially an elaboration and extension of an idea by repeating that idea in many different figures of speech. It is akin to *commoratio* (dwelling upon) but is more elaborate and descriptive.

Shakespeare uses the device in *The Winter's Tale*:

> I take thy hand—this hand,
> As soft as dove's down and as white as it,
> Or Ethiopian's tooth, or the fann'd snow
>   that's bolted
> By the northern blasts twice o'er.

A contemporary writer uses the device in this way:

Sheet upon sheet of blazing yellow, half way between sulphur and celadine, with hot golden sunshine pouring down upon them out of a dazzling June sky. It thrilled me like music.

—Monica Baldwin

It has been said that we feed the hungry, clothe the naked, bind up the wounds of the man beaten by thieves, pour oil and wine into them, set him on our own beast and bring him to the inn, because we receive ourselves pleasure from these acts.

—Thomas Jefferson

. . . swollen in head, weak in legs, sharp in tongue but empty in belly.

—Mao Tse-Tung's description of intellectuals

A man should be taller, older, heavier, uglier, and hoarser than his wife.

—E. W. Howe

Fleur's wisdom in refusing to write to him was profound, for he reached each new place entirely without hope or fervor, and could concentrate immediate attention on the donkeys and tumbling bells, the priests, patios, beggars, children, crowing cocks, sombreros, cactus-hedges, old high white villages, goats, olive-trees, greening plains, singing birds in tiny cages, water-sellers, sunsets, melons, mules, great churches, pictures, and swimming grey-brown mountains of a fascinating land.

—John Galsworthy

. . . Twenty years after, on the other side of the globe, again the filth of murky foxholes, the stench of ghostly trenches, the slime of dripping dugouts, those boiling suns of the relentless heat, those torrential rains of devastating storms, the loneliness and utter desolation of jungle trails, the bitterness of long separation from those they loved and cherished, and the deadly pestilence of tropical disease, the horror of stricken areas of war.

—Douglas MacArthur

A device with a similar effect was what the Greeks called *synathroesmus* meaning "collection," also known as *congeries*, "a heap." Here you pile up adjectives.

This one-cylinder Barnum, this tower of sneers in tasseled shoes, this Shubert Alley Catiline, this mustachioed-thane of the sceptered aisle, this Greek god, this other Edam, this papier-mache genius, this blessed plotter, this doozer producer, this publicity addict who would send his cocker spaniel to Cape Canaveral if he thought it would get into space, this man, this David Merrick has done it again.

—*Time* magazine

There are dancing rooms and dining rooms; listening rooms and talking rooms. . . . Big rooms, small rooms, banquet rooms, ballrooms . . . Pink rooms, red rooms, blue rooms, bedrooms . . . Fun rooms, sun rooms, old rooms, new rooms; altogether, six hundred and two rooms.

—*Town & Country,* of the St. Regis Hotel, New York, 1963

This is the way one advertiser uses the device:

City car, suburban car, second car, only car, mother car, bachelor car, college car, family car, near car, far car, the car, the fun car from France!

—Renault

VI

FIGURES OF THOUGHT

THE TERM "FIGURE OF THOUGHT" WAS USED IN CLASSICAL rhetoric to define a large-scale trope or scheme, or a combination of both, such as an allegory. We use the term to encompass those devices that involve a pattern of ideas rather than merely a pattern of words.

The simplest of all the devices you can use to make an expression distinctive and memorable is one that requires, more than others, ego rather than great literary talent. In fact it has a sort of ego of its own. Here you exploit the fact that a statement made with authority and seeming logic receives more attention than one made in more ordinary prose.

IN SHORT FORM

One of the most effective figures of thought is the slogan, which the Romans called *brevitas*, "shortness," or "concise statement." It is designed to be so striking that truth or falsity becomes almost irrelevant. Its impact may be limitless. A nation's history may be molded by a slogan. It becomes the advertising gimmick of a government that may express and shape the philosophy of a nation for years—Roosevelt's New Deal, Kennedy's New Frontier, Johnson's Great Society, are all slogans that summed up in a pithy phrase the ideals and ideas of a particular administration. Slogans have played a large role in political affairs:

Isolationism is dead.

—Harry S Truman

Food will win the war.

—Herbert Hoover

Don't tread on me.
　　　　　—Used with drawing of a rattlesnake as a flag
　　　　　for the colonists early in the American
　　　　　Revolution, 1775 and 1776

Remember the Alamo!
　　　　　—Texas battle cry in its war with Mexico

Remember the Maine.
　　—Slogan of the Spanish-American War prompted by
　　the mysterious explosion of the battleship at
　　Havana which had much to do with U.S. intervention

Remember Pearl Harbor.

It can't happen here.

—Sinclair Lewis

The full dinner pail.

—McKinley-Roosevelt ticket, 1900

Turn the rascals out.

—Charles A. Dana

We shall overcome.

—Civil rights movement, 1960s

The slogan is often an accident of oratory:

The only safe rule is to promise little, and faithfully to keep every promise; to speak softly and carry a big stick.

—Theodore Roosevelt

Our whole duty, for the present, at any rate, is summed up in the motto: "America first."

—Woodrow Wilson

The State cannot get a cent for any man without taking it from some other man. . . . The latter is the Forgotten Man.

—William Graham Sumner

I pledge you, I pledge myself, to a new deal for the American people.

—Franklin D. Roosevelt

Brevity has been used effectively in other ways for similar impact:

To hell with you. Offensive letter follows.

—Irate citizen's telegram quoted by
Lord Home, Britain's Foreign Secretary

EPIGRAMS, MAXIMS, PROVERBS

The epigram is brief, but more extensive than the slogan. It was originally conceived as a short poem with a surprise turn of thought or a witty statement at the end. The form was two to six lines in length, ending with a sting in the last two lines.

Webster's Third gives as an example the poem by John Wilmot, Earl of Rochester, about Charles II.

> Here lies our sovereign lord the King,
> Whose word no man relies on;
> He never says a foolish thing,
> Nor ever does a wise one.

Here are two of the older variety by a specialist, J. Walthof, 1737:

> A humorous fellow in a tavern late,
> Being drunk and valiant, gets a broken pate;
> The surgeon, with his instruments and skill,

> Searches his skull, deeper and deeper still,
> To feel his brains; and try if they were found;
> And, as he keeps ado about the wound,
> The fellow calls, "Good surgeon spare your pains
> When I began this brawl I had no brains."

Of a hung picture:

> See how she blooms, even when her autumn's past!
> And a complexion does command,
> Due only to her skillful hand;
> Her hand, which in an hour repairs
> The injuries of sixty years.

The epigram, for the most part, lost its rhyme and meter and became merely a terse, wise, witty statement, sometimes citing a paradox. Oscar Levant once defined it as "a wisecrack that played Carnegie Hall."

When the epigram assumed the proportion of being a general truth, it became known as a *maxim* (from the Latin "greatest proposition"), or *apothegm* (from the Greek "terse saying"), or a *proverb* or *adage* (from the Latin "old saying"), or a *gnome* (from the Greek "thought or judgment") or *sententia* (from the Latin "judgment"). One distinction widely accepted is that an epigram is coined by a person whose name we know, while a proverb evolves from common usage.

Apothegms and maxims are based on the wisdom of one person; proverbs and adages on the wisdom of a community. Of these, the proverb carries the greatest authority. But no law prohibits anyone from making a "profound" judgment.

All are terse, pointed, often witty statements, usually with a sense of authority. All have become collectors' items.

One of the most well-known of epigrammatists was the seventeenth-century writer La Rochefoucauld. Here are a few of his maxims, which sum up a great deal of thought in a few effective words:

Our virtues are most frequently but vices in disguise.

We give nothing more generously than advice.

The love of justice in most men is simply the fear of suffering injustice.

Oscar Wilde, of course, was famous for his witty epigrams, which often employed paradox, a seemingly self-contradictory statement:

Conscience and cowardice are really the same things.

In this world there are only two tragedies. One is not getting what one wants, and the other is getting it.

Experience is the name everyone gives to their mistakes.

Your epigrams and maxims do not necessarily have to be witty or paradoxical. Here are some examples that make serious statements concisely:

Necessity is the mother of invention.

Experience is the mother of science.

Change is the law of life.

Great causes are never tried on their merits.
—Ralph Waldo Emerson

We are wiser than we know.
—Ralph Waldo Emerson

Knowledge is the antidote to fear . . .
—William Hazlitt

That man is the richest whose pleasures are the cheapest.
—Henry David Thoreau

UP AND DOWN

Another way you can make your words more effective is to present them in climactic order. You start with your least important idea and build up to your most important. Climax, in other words, is achieved by arranging your ideas so that they gradually increase in significance. The word *climax* itself comes from the Greek word meaning "ladder." In Latin it is called *gradatio* or *ascendus*. Puttenham called it *marching figure*. Thomas Wilson in *The Arte of Rhetorique* (1553) gives as an example:

Labour getteth learning, learning getteth fame,
fame getteth honour, honour getteth bliss forever.

Climaxes can be logical, emotional, chronological, or simply numerical.

A logical climax depends on reasoning, contrast, or a similar thought process to reach a conclusion:

A sound body is good; a sound mind is better; but a strong and clean character is better than either.

—Theodore Roosevelt

The only gracious way to accept an insult is to ignore it; if you can't ignore it, top it; if you can't top it, laugh at it; if you can't laugh at it, it's probably deserved.

—Russell Lynes, *Reader's Digest,* 1961

The emotional climax, on the other hand, builds on words with certain connotations, or is patterned on the expression of feelings:

It was a lovely city, a beautiful city, a fair city, a veritable gem of a city.

He was pleased when the child began to adventure across floors on hands and knees; he was gratified when she managed the trick of balancing herself on two legs; he was delighted when she first said "ta-ta"; and he was rejoiced when she recognized him and smiled at him.

—Alan Paton

Nobody ever stopped him in the street to say, with gladsome looks, "My dear Scrooge, how are you? When will you come to see me?" No beggars implored him to bestow a trifle, no children asked him what it was o'clock, no man or woman ever once in all his life inquired the way to such and such a place, of Scrooge. Even the blind men's dogs appeared to know him, and when they saw him coming on, would tug their owners into doorways and up courts; and then would wag their tails, as though they said, "No eye at all is better than an evil eye, dark master!"

—Charles Dickens

> I pray that I may not be married
> but if I am to be married
> that I may not be a cuckold
> but if I am to be a cuckold
> that I may not know it
> but if I am to know
> that I may not mind.
> —"The Bachelor's Prayer," 1630

The chronological climax is achieved by tracing an action over a period of time:

Little by little, bit by bit, day by day and year by year, the baron got the worst of some disputed question.

—Charles Dickens

Out of our beliefs are born deeds. Out of our deeds we form habits; out of our habits grow our character; and on our character we build our destination.

—Dean Henry Hancock, St. Mark's Cathedral

These are some examples of the use of climax from historic occasions:

This is a Senate of equals, of men of individual honor and personal character, and of absolute independence. We know no masters; we acknowledge no dictators.

—Daniel Webster

Let every nation know, whether it wishes us well or ill, that we shall pay any price, bear any burden, meet any hardship, support any friend, oppose any foe in order to assure the survival and success of liberty.

—John F. Kennedy

Be civil to all; sociable to many; familiar with few; friend to one; enemy to none.

—Benjamin Franklin

And, for the support of this declaration, with a firm reliance on the protection of Divine Providence, we mutually pledge to each other our lives, our fortunes, and our sacred honor.

—Declaration of Independence

There is no right to strike against the public safety by anybody, anywhere, any time.

—Calvin Coolidge as Governor of Massachusetts, to Samuel Gompers, of a strike by the Boston police, 1919

If there was a general election tomorrow the Socialist majority would vanish. If they wait another year, they themselves will vanish for a considerable period, "unwept, unhonoured, and unsung—and unhung."

—Winston Churchill

ANTICLIMAX

One way of enlivening your writing or speeches is to build suspense by leading your audience along a significant or dignified line of thought—and then suddenly ending on a trivial note. The Greeks called this *bathos*, literally, "depth"; a thought "sinks" from the elevated to the commonplace. Anticlimax involves a building up of tension followed by an unexpected denouement or ending. It is the basis of much of contemporary American humor.

She was, and in my mind's eye, she still is, a thing of quivering beauty. Quivering? Undeniably. Beautiful? To me, unutterably. She was my first motor-car.

—John Marshall

Small children are fascinated by flowers. They can't wait to see them come up—roots and all.

—Bob Brown

The most important thing a father can do for his children is to love their mother.

—Rev. Theodore Hesburgh

Valentine's Day is approaching, a time to recall that your wife still likes candy and flowers. Show her you remember, by speaking of them occasionally.

—Earl Wilson

The tanned appearance of many Londoners is not sunburn—it is rust.

—London *Evening Standard*

I asked a Burmese why women, after centuries of following their men, now walked ahead. He said there were many unexploded land mines since the war.

—Robert Mueller

When I was a young man I vowed never to marry until I found the ideal woman. Well, I found her—but, alas, she was waiting for the ideal man.

—Robert Schuman, French Foreign Minister

The best way I know of to win an argument is to start by being in the right.

—Quinton Hogg, Lord Hailsham

Annette got rid of 215 pounds of excessively flabby fat in 90 days. She divorced him.

For twenty years my wife and I were ecstatically happy. . . . Then we met.

AND ACROSS

Chiasmus is a sort of reverse parallel construction. In it, you repeat a pattern with a cross order of words and phrases. Thus you invert the structure or word order of one sentence juxtaposed with another.

> As high as we have mounted in delight.
> In our defection do we send us low.
> —William Wordsworth

Though the people support the Government, the Government should not support the people.

—Grover Cleveland

To add life to years, not just years to life.

A wit with dunces, and a dunce with wits.

—Alexander Pope

ANTITHESIS

Antithesis from the Greek "opposition," was a formal figure of speech that ranked in importance with the metaphor, and it is one of the oldest in literature. It makes its point by finding areas of contrast.

Through the years it has been called variously *antitheton, contentio, contraposition*, and *opposita*. Here you simply put together opposite concepts or ideas. Puttenham called it *quarreller*.

A saint abroad, and a devil at home.

—George Gordon Lord Byron

Better to reign in hell than serve in heav'n.

—Lucifer, John Milton's *Paradise Lost*

Actually there are two types of antithesis: You can use contrasting words or use contrasting ideas. The beginning of *A Tale of Two Cities* is an example that depends on the use of antonyms.

It was the best of times, it was the worst of times, it was the age of wisdom, it was the age of foolishness, it was the epoch of belief, it was the epoch of incredulity, it was the season of Light, it was the season of Darkness, it was the spring of hope, it was the winter of despair, we had everything before us, we had nothing before us, we were all going direct to Heaven, we are all going direct the other way . . .

—Charles Dickens

An advertiser uses it this way:

Someone is telling your kids very bad lies about a very good gum.

—Bubble Yum

Contrasting ideas are presented similarly:

Nothing is so commonplace as to wish to be remarkable.

—Oliver Wendell Holmes

In this age when there can be no losers in peace and no victors in war, we must recognize the obligation to match national strength with national restraint.

—Lyndon B. Johnson

There is only one thing in the world worse than being talked about, and that is not being talked about.

—Oscar Wilde

With public sentiment, nothing can fail; without it, nothing can succeed.

—Abraham Lincoln

He that is of the opinion money will do everything may well be suspected of doing everything for money.

—Benjamin Franklin

Faith is to believe what we do not see; and the reward of this faith is to see what we believe.

—St. Augustine

CONTRAST

Contrasting component parts of an expression is common to many rhetorical devices. Probably the most elemental is to bring together heterogeneous unrelated elements in a way that indicates they are equal in rank or part of the same class. Thus you can put together literary and colloquial words, words of science and of poetry, and so forth, creating a literary shock that forces the reader to stop to consider the meaning. In such juxtaposition, one or both of the elements take on a slightly different meaning. Here are some applications:

Contrast in imagery is frequently utilized by Lord Byron in *Don Juan*:

> But oh? Ambrosial cash! Oh who would lose thee?
> When we no more can use, or even abuse thee.

And again:

> Let us have work and women, mirth and laughter,
> Sermons and soda water—the day after!

And again:

> They grieved for those who perished with the cutter
> And also for the biscuit casks and butter.

> He loved philosophy and a good dinner.
> . . . his tutor and his spaniel

Contrast in style is typified by this line from Somerset Maugham's "The Hour Before the Dawn":

Will you oblige me by keeping your trap shut, darling.

An advertising copywriter uses the device in this way:

Proven thick by spoon and spouse.

—Hunt's tomato paste

And:

Democracy does not come in a plain brown wrapper.

—North American Publishing Company

Moe Ginsburg's
  Spectacular
Presidential Sale

One method is simply bringing together concepts not usually associated. Thus, some well-known book titles:

The Insolent Chariots
    —by John Keats, 1958 book about the automobile

The Rich and Other Atrocities
        —by Charlotte Curtis, 1976

Modern Man Is Obsolete
        —by Norman Cousins, 1945

The Engineering of Consent
        —by Edward Bernays

Idiot's Delight
        —by Robert Sherwood

Some other examples:

The future of the past.

—*The New York Times*

"Patience is action"

—by Marianne Moore

And in a comment:

Success has ruined many a man.

—Benjamin Franklin

Comparing contrary elements in contrasting clauses— called *syncrisis*, "comparison" in Greek, and *dissimilitude*, "unlikeness" in Latin—is a variation of antithesis:

He who has a thousand friends has not a friend to spare
And he who has one enemy will meet him everywhere.

—Ralph Waldo Emerson

For every right that you cherish, you have a duty which you must fulfill. For every hope that you entertain, you have a task you must perform. For every good that you wish to preserve, you will have to sacrifice your comfort and ease. There is nothing for nothing any longer.

—Walter Lippmann, 1940

With people of only moderate ability modesty is mere honesty; but with those who possess great talent it is hypocrisy.

—Arthur Schopenhauer

The bee that hath honey in her mouth hath a sting in her tail.

—John Lyly

When we assumed the soldier, we did not lay aside the citizen.

—George Washington

The United States never lost a war or won a conference.

—Will Rogers

It is the province of knowledge to speak and it is the privilege of wisdom to listen.

—Oliver Wendell Holmes

Burn down your cities and leave our farms, and your cities will spring up again; but destroy our farms and the grass will grow in the streets of every city in the country.

—William Jennings Bryan

I have said to the people we mean to have less government in business as well as more business in government.

—Warren G. Harding

Contemporary advertisers put it this way:

Why turn on the water when the water can turn you on?

—Water Pik

It's great to be big.
It's bigger to be great.

—Lerman & Van Leeuwen, Inc.

THE CARROUSEL

The carrousel is a kind of rhetorical merry-go-round that you can often use for humorous effect. By linking one idea to the next by repetition or by simple logic you get a chain of thoughts that ultimately comes full circle. This device can be useful in pointing out the absurdity of an idea or an institution.

With progress in roads came more cars, more roads for the cars, and more cars for the roads that had been built to accommodate more cars.

—*Time,* report on U.S. Highways, 1961

If you do things merely because you think some other fool expects you to do them, and he expects you to do them because he thinks you expect him to expect you to do them, it will end in everybody doing what nobody wants to do, which is in my opinion a silly state of things.

—George Bernard Shaw

No well-bred European girl would chat with a stranger on a bus or if she did, wouldn't date him the same day or if she did, she wouldn't bring him home; or if she did her parents would have a fit.

—Hans Konigsberger

God makes the grass, the air and the rain; and the grass, the air and the rain made the Irish; and the Irish turned the grass, the air and the rain back to God.

—Sean O'Faolain

Broadway is a place where people spend money they haven't earned to buy things they don't need to impress people they don't like.

—Walter Winchell

Here's to the men!
When I meet 'em, I like 'em.
When I like 'em, I kiss 'em.
When I kiss 'em, I love 'em.
When I love 'em, I let 'em.
When I let 'em, I lose 'em.
God-damn 'em!

INCONSISTENCIES

A combination of words with inconsistent meanings that are either directly or almost directly opposite or contradictory is called an *oxymoron*, from the Greek meaning "a witty, paradoxical saying." A common example is "wise fool." Such expressions as "perfectly awful," "proud humility," "deafening silence," "such sweet sorrow," and "pleasant rascal" are oxymorons. O. Henry used it effectively in describing New York:

I despise its very vastness and power. It has the poorest millionaires, the littlest great men, the haughtiest beggars, the plainest beauties, the lowest skyscrapers, the dolefulest pleasures of any town I ever saw.

PARADOX

Paradox, from the Greek meaning "contrary to opinion or expectation," (called *wondrer* by Puttenham) involves a statement that appears to contradict itself. Paradox is based on apparently sane premises that yield an incongruous or inconvenient conclusion that is nevertheless perhaps true.

We are faced with the paradoxical fact that education has become one of the chief obstacles to intelligence and freedom of thought.
—Bertrand Russell

A man in love is incomplete until he has married. Then he's finished.
—Zsa Zsa Gabor

This is the only country that ever went to the poorhouse in an automobile.
—Will Rogers

All the rivers run into the sea; yet the sea is not full.
—Ecclesiastes 1:7

It is well that war is so terrible—we would grow too fond of it.
—General Robert E. Lee

That which is called firmness in a king is called obstinacy in a donkey.
—Thomas Erskine

Silence is one great art of conversation.
—William Hazlitt

It is odd that one of the keys to abundance should have been handed to civilization on a platter of destruction.
—Adlai Stevenson

One of the best ways to persuade others is with your ears—by listening to them.

—Dean Rusk

If our air forces are never used, they have achieved their first goal.

—General Nathan Twining

I have made this letter longer than usual because I lack the time to make it shorter.

—Pascal

Israel Government Tourist Office uses the device in this way:

After forty centuries, it's great to be thirty.

THE IRRELEVANT

A witty paradox is often based on emphasizing the irrelevant:

When a man points a finger at someone else, he should remember that four of his fingers are pointing at himself.

—Louis Nizer

The long and distressing controversy over capital punishment is very unfair to anyone meditating murder.

—Geoffrey Fisher

He recited Lincoln's Gettysburg Address and he's only 8. Lincoln didn't do it until he was 50.

—Earl Wilson quoting Mark Gerdi

Those who warn of a population explosion picture a world of too many people and not enough food—sort of like the average cocktail party.

—Bill Vaughn

The most common impediment of speech in children is bubble gum.

—Roger Allen

Speak well of your enemies; after all, you made them.

And an old joke:

Teacher: "This is the fifth time I've had to punish you this week. What have you to say, Samuel?"
Samuel: "I'm glad it's Friday!"

Often the basis of paradox is anomaly or anachronism. An anomaly is simply an irregularity, something inconsistent with normal expectations. An anachronism is, in a sense, a special kind of anomaly. It involves something that is chronologically incongruous or misplaced. When you use an anomaly or an anachronism unintentionally, it can be ludicrous, but when you use it on purpose, it can be witty and help to make a point. The Greeks had a term, *anacoluthon*, translated as "anomalous" or "inconsistent," which had a similar use.

Nostalgia isn't what it used to be.

—Peter De Vries, *Reader's Digest*

Even the future is not what it used to be.

. . . something like wearing a three-cornered hat with an Ivy League suit.

—New York *Herald Tribune* of a Jacqueline Kennedy dinner

I feel it is time that I also pay tribute to my four writers, Matthew, Mark, Luke and John.

—Bishop Fulton J. Sheen on receiving award for his television show

The modern home is going to be equipped with the latest in domestic kitchen appliances. You press a button and it lights the gas by rubbing two sticks together.

Bad officials are the ones elected by good citizens who do not vote.

—George Jean Nathan

It is one of the ironies of life that when one grows tall enough to reach the jam on the pantry shelf, the craving for jam has left.

—*Purdue Agriculturist*

We are getting to the point where we know that a great many of our secrets are known to the enemy, but they are still secret from our friends, which seems to be a rather anomalous situation.

—Dwight D. Eisenhower, on revision of security laws

DEFINITION

The definition is one of the most effective ways to present an idea. It is a short, direct way to clarify a thought. The simplest way to define something, of course, is to give a synonym, but you can also make a definition by putting the word to be defined into a larger class of things, by saying what it is not, and by giving the meaning a new and clever twist that goes beyond the mere dictionary definition. Here are several formats:

To me, old age is always fifteen years older than I am.

—Bernard Baruch, on his eighty-fifth birthday

A statesman is a successful politician who is dead.

—Thomas Brackett Reed

What do you call a man who doesn't believe in birth control? Daddy.

Refugees—People who vote with their feet.

—*Berliner Illustrierte,* of crowds fleeing Communist Germany, 1961

Prejudice: A vagrant opinion without visible means of support.

—Ambrose Bierce

A bigot is anyone who is obstinately and zealously attached to an opinion that you do not agree with.

Intuition is suspicion in skirts.

Small gifts are charity; big gifts are philanthropy.

If you can sell someone something he doesn't want at a price he can't afford, that's salesmanship.

Geography can be defined as "What on earth!"

Now as to politeness . . . I would venture to call it benevolence in trifles.

—William Pitt, Earl of Chatham

When a man sits with a pretty girl for an hour, it seems like a minute. But let him sit on a hot stove for a minute—and it's longer than any hour. That's relativity.

—Albert Einstein

A diplomat is a person who can tell you to go to hell in such a way that you actually look forward to the trip.

—Caskie Stinnett

Culture is what your butcher would have if he were a surgeon.

—Mary Pettibone Poole

What is history but a fable agreed upon?

—Napoleon

A liberal is a man who is willing to spend somebody else's money.

—Carter Glass

An advertiser uses the device in this way:

Happiness is getting a big fat check every month during retirement.

Pure joy is getting a nice big tax credit each year until you retire.

—New York Bank for Savings

You can use definition to state a truth that is so self-evident that people tend not to realize its veracity until it is pointed out to them:

Today is the first day of the rest of your life.

A journey of 10,000 miles begins with the first step.

Don't let life discourage you; everyone who got where he is had to begin where he was.

—Richard L. Evans

One man's telephone number is another man's wrong number.

One man's terrorist is another man's freedom fighter . . .

—*The New York Times*

It is difference of opinion that makes horse-races.

—Mark Twain

The hole and the patch should be commensurate.

—Thomas Jefferson

Popularity is a matter of opinion.

There is a budding morrow in the midnight.

—John Keats

Or less obvious:

Discontent is the first step in the progress of a man or a nation.

—Oscar Wilde

Often you'll find it more effective to emphasize the distinction rather than the definition:

No people is wholly civilized where a distinction is drawn between stealing an office and stealing a purse.
—Theodore Roosevelt

A politician is a person with whose politics you don't agree. If you agree with him, he is a statesman.
—David Lloyd George

Simply making the distinction between words is another device.

Your old men shall dream dreams; your young men shall see visions.
—Joel, 2:28

A speech need not be eternal to be immortal.

Most advocates of realism are in this world hopelessly unrealistic.
—Jawaharlal Nehru

Gray hair is a sign of age, not of wisdom.
—Greek proverb

When a man wants to murder a tiger, he calls it sport; when the tiger wants to murder him he calls it ferocity. The distinction between crime and justice is no greater.
—George Bernard Shaw

By "radical" I understand one who goes too far; by "conservative" one who does not go far enough; by "reactionary" one who won't go at all.
—Woodrow Wilson

The only difference between a rut and a grave is their dimensions.
—Ellen Glasgow

In an advertisement:

The difference between good and great . . .
—Seagram's 7 Crown

The denigrating definition or a metaphor used to degrade or humiliate (the Greeks used the term *tapinosis* for such expressions) is often created by definition. Thus a writer may become a phrasemonger, a poet, a rhymester, a statesman, a politician.

The pejorative effect is easily created:

A radical is a man with both feet firmly planted in the air.
—Franklin D. Roosevelt

Conservatism is the policy of "make no change and consult your grandmother when in doubt."
—Woodrow Wilson

A fanatic is one who can't change his mind and won't change the subject.
—Winston Churchill

A critic is a legless man who teaches running.
—Channing Pollock (1880–1946), *The Green Book*

Doctors are men who prescribe medicines of which they know little, to cure diseases of which they know less, in human beings of whom they know nothing.
—Voltaire

A diplomat is one who can cut his neighbor's throat without having his neighbor notice it.
—Trygve Lie

A contradiction in terms is a marriage of definition and paradox.

All animals are equal, but some are more equal than others.
—George Orwell, *Animal Farm*

In wartime, I said, "Truth is so precious that she should always be attended by a bodyguard of lies."

—Winston Churchill

Let us all be happy and live within our means, even if we have to borrow money to do it with.

—Artemus Ward

In heaven an angel is nobody in particular.

—George Bernard Shaw

I have come to the conclusion that politics are too serious a matter to be left to the politicians.

—Charles de Gaulle

Youth is a wonderful thing. What a crime to waste it on children.

—George Bernard Shaw

I am free of all prejudice. I hate everyone equally.

—W. C. Fields

The United Nations is a good idea, but it's too bad we have to have so many foreigners in it.

You can't get there from here.

I am an atheist, thank God.

The worst cliques are those that consist of one man.

—George Bernard Shaw

I can resist everything except temptation.

—Oscar Wilde

RATIOS

The same term, analogy, or *proportio*, which is one of the original tropes, applies to a different type of expression—the ratio.

Feminine passion is to masculine as an epic is to an epigram.

—Karl Kraus

BY THE NUMBERS

Enumeration strikes a subliminal chord of credence. Perhaps because we are brought up on ABC's and 1-2-3's we accept enumeration as evidence of truth. Rhetorically, enumerations put separate elements into a chain of homogeneous links. The relationship of the elements you choose may be one of cause and effect, of chronology, of similarity or dissimilarity, of logical sequence, of proximity, or of subjective personal experience. The Romans, inevitably, had a term for this: *enumeratio*.

Here is an example of enumeration showing a cause and effect relationship:

Italians come to ruin most generally in three ways, women, gambling, and farming. My family chose the slowest one.

—Pope John XXIII

Chronology:

At twenty years of age the will reigns; at thirty the wit; at forty the judgment.

—Benjamin Franklin

Who at twenty knows nothing, at thirty does nothing, at forty has nothing.

—Italian proverb

Telling lies is a fault in a boy, an art in a lover, an accomplishment in a bachelor, and second nature in a married woman.

—Helen Rowland

Every great scientific truth goes through three stages. First, people say it conflicts with the Bible. Next, they say it has been discovered before. Lastly, they say they have always believed it.

—Louis Agassiz

Yesterday is experience. Tomorrow is hope. Today is getting from one to the other as best we can.

—Baxter Springs

Similarity:

We have accepted . . . a second Bill of Rights under which a new basis of security and prosperity can be established for all —regardless of station, race or creed. Among these are: The right of a useful and remunerative job in the industries or shops or farms or mines of the Nation:

The right to earn enough to provide adequate food and clothing and recreation.

The right of every farmer to raise and sell his products at a return which will give him and his family a decent living.

The right of every businessman, large and small, to trade in an atmosphere of freedom from unfair competition and domination by monopolies at home or abroad.

The right of every family to a decent home.

The right to adequate medical care and the opportunity to achieve and enjoy good health.

The right to adequate protection from the economic fears of old age, sickness, accident, and unemployment.

The right to a good education.

All of these spell security.

—Franklin D. Roosevelt

Dissimilarity:

Some women blush when they are kissed; some call for the police; some swear; some bite. But the worst are those who laugh.

He who will not reason is a bigot;
He who cannot is a fool;
And he who dares not is a slave.

—William Drummond

Frustrate a Frenchman, he will drink himself to death; an Irishman, he will die of angry hypertension; a Dane, he will shoot himself; an American, he will get drunk, shoot you, then establish a million dollar aid program for your relatives. Then he will die of an ulcer.

—Dr. Stanley Rudin, psychologist

Logical sequence:

> Three things the speaker should remember.
> Be good
> Be brief
> Be seated.

A timid person is frightened before a danger, a coward during the time, and a courageous person afterwards.

—Jean-Paul Richter

Proximity:

There are three faithful friends—an old wife, an old dog, and ready money.

—Benjamin Franklin

Subjective order:

> How do I love thee? Let me count the ways.
> I love thee to the depth and breadth and height
> My soul can reach, when feeling out of sight
> For the ends of Being, and ideal Grace. . . .

—Elizabeth Barrett Browning

There are three marks of a superior man: being virtuous, he is free from anxiety; being wise, he is free from perplexity; being brave, he is free from fear.

—Confucius

An advertising use:

Four essentials of business: people, capital, plant, and Dun & Bradstreet.

Similarly, division or distribution—given the name *merismus* by the Greeks and *divisio* by the Romans—consists of dividing a subject into parts:

The world is divided into two classes of people: the few people who make good on their promises (even if they don't promise too much) and the many who don't.

—Robert Townsend

There is, for many people, strong acceptance of even a number itself as verification. Thus:

The Ten Commandments
The Twelve Tablets
The Seven Wonders of the World
The Ten Great Victories for Freedom

Here they are used to advantage:

Ten rules for getting rid of the blues: Go out and do something for someone else. And repeat it nine times.

And in a more direct vein:

People buy their first bottle of Charbaut champagne because of the price. They buy their second bottle because of the first.

—A. Charbaut & Fils

A boy has two jobs. One is just being a boy. The other is growing up to be a man.

—Herbert Hoover to the Boys' Club

In her opinion, the seven ages of a woman are: baby, infant, junior miss, young woman, young woman, young woman, young woman. It is difficult to live in the present, ridiculous to live in the future, and impossible to live in the past. Nothing is as far away as one minute ago.

—Jim Bishop

There are four things, which, I humbly conceive, are essential to the well-being, I may even venture to say, to the existence of the United States . . .

1st. An indissoluble Union of the States under one Federal head.
2nd. A sacred regard to Public Justice.

3rd. The adoption of a proper Peace Establishment, and
4th. The prevalence of that pacific and friendly Disposition,
among the people of the United States, which will induce
them to forget their local prejudices and policies, to make
those mutual concessions which are requisite to the general
prosperity, and in some instances, to sacrifice their individual
advantages to the interest of the Community.
These are the Pillars on which the glorious Fabrick of our
independency and National Character must be supported.
—George Washington, Circular to the Governors, 1783

She talks 80% faster than anyone can listen.

This is how advertisers use the device:

March 1, 1977: The day all Los Angeles started to get relief
from welfare.
—Sperry-Rand Corporation

The girl you love is 70.2% water.
—McCann Erickson advertising agency

51 Ways to find room at the top.
—Business Week

Creating a formula is an elementary device you can easily
adapt to almost any situation.

Success is that old ABC—ability, breaks and courage.
—Charles Luckman

One might risk establishing the following mathematical formula
for bribery, namely OG=PLRXAEB: The opportunity for graft
equals the plethora of legal requirements multiplied by the
number of architects, engineers and builders.
—Harold Birns, New York City Building Commissioner

If A equals success, then the formula A equals X plus Y plus
Z. X is work. Y is play. Z is keep your mouth shut.
—Albert Einstein

One thousand dollars invested in salvaging an unemployable youth today can return forty thousand dollars in his lifetime.

—Lyndon Johnson

They call her "A. T. & T."—Always Talking and Talking.

Here are some examples used in contemporary advertising:

Can $1 = 4$?

—Duracell

My personality is ph 6.5—just slightly on the acid side.

And a comment on advertising itself:

Advertising is 85% confusion and 15% commission.

—Fred Allen

CHAPTER

NEGATIVE, ANODYNE, AND AVOIDANCE DEVICES

MANY RHETORICAL DEVICES ARE MORE NOTEWORTHY FOR what they do not permit to be said than for what is said, for denial or avoidance rather than for assertion. Such figures can involve understatement, faint praise or faint condemnation, ambiguity, innuendo, sarcasm, irony, euphemisms, circumlocution, pomposity, bombast, and sometimes sheer nonsense. Obviously, these techniques have an important place in communication. And, of course, the Greeks had words for most of them.

Just as military tactics are not limited to a frontal attack, we recognize that not every point is best made by a direct statement. There are times when the less said the better, when saying nothing, avoiding the question, being ambiguous or indirect, diverting or obfuscating are your best weapons. And there are times when saying what you do not mean is the best way to convey a message.

An apocryphal story is credited to Marine General O. P. Smith. During the Korean War he responded to a taunt about pulling back: "Retreating, hell, we're just advancing backward." In rhetoric there are many ways of advancing backward.

UNDERSTATEMENT

Litotes, from the Greek meaning "plainness, simplicity," is a form of understatement expressed by the denial of the contrary. The Romans recognized this technique as *diminútio*, meaning "lessening," sometimes called *exadversio*, meaning "opposition," and sometimes *tenuitas*, "smallness." Puttenham called it *moderatour*. The idea behind litotes is that a double negative makes a positive. By occasionally using this device, you can vary your style and frequently intensify the impact of an understatement. A classic example is: "He likes his wife not a little" for "he dotes on her."

But we need not look far to find such expressions as:

He does not starve himself.

It is no small task.

It is no less important.

Not entirely without humor . . .

She was no country cousin.

Or expressions that actually do use double negatives:

He was not entirely displeased.

It is not unusual . . .

It is not unlike the American system.

Your use may be more elaborate. As a candidate for prime minister, asked about the concern voiced by some Israeli officials that the United States might be about to attempt to impose a settlement, Mr. Shimon Peres replied:

The fact that there are worried people is not strange to me.

Understatement is not really characteristic of Americans,

but the British are renowned for it. The Greeks called under-statement that belittles or makes something seem less important *meiosis*, meaning "lessening," and the Romans *imminutio*, which has about the same meaning, and Puttenham called it *disabler*.

> The English sporting instinct is inexhaustible. When a body is found bearing ninety-six hatchet wounds, a bullet in the heart and a pound of arsenic in the stomach the British police do not so much as breathe the word murder. Instead, they suspect foul play, which is more than sporting of them in the circumstances.
> —Mesentente Cordiale

> We have reason to believe you have committed an offence.
> —John Crosby, on a London police ticket
> for overtime parking

Newsweek once described the Madison Avenue definition of death:

> Nature's way of telling you to slow down.

The device is not limited to the British or to mystery stories. From two of the world's richest men:

> Well, yes, you could say we have independent means.
> —John D. Rockefeller, Jr.

> Thanks a thousand.
> —Nelson Rockefeller, a "conservative" expression

> A billion here, a billion there . . . after a while that begins to be real money.
> —Everett Dirksen

> I've been rich and I've been poor. Rich is better.
> —Sophie Tucker

Or, more elaborately:

> Dying is bad for you.
> —Russell Baker

I do not see any way of realizing our hopes about world organization in five or six days. Even the Almighty took seven.

—Winston Churchill

There are variations:

After all what was *Medea*? Just another child custody case.

—Frank Pierşen, *The New York Times*

Although always prepared for martyrdom, I preferred that it should be postponed.

—George Bernard Shaw

The counterpart is overstatement to a point of being ridiculous:

I note what you say about your aspiration to edit a magazine. I am sending you by this mail a six-chambered revolver. Load it and fire every one into your head. You will thank me after you get to Hell and learn from other editors how dreadful their job was on earth. I wouldn't go back to magazine editing for all the money wasted by the Brain Trust.

—H. L. Mencken to William Saroyan, 1936

And, more simply:

If I shoot at the sun I might hit a star.

—P. T. Barnum

FAINT PRAISE

Damning with faint praise is a well-known device. A not-so-recent famous comment with more than a little sarcasm:

Miss Truman is a unique American phenomenon with a pleasant voice of little size and fair quality . . . yet Miss Truman cannot sing very well. She is flat a good deal of the time . . . she communicates almost nothing of the music she presents. . . . There are few moments during her recital when one can relax and feel confident that she will make her goal, which is the end of the song.

—Paul Hume, music critic of the *Washington Post*

To which, incidentally, her father the President responded:

> I have just read your lousy review buried in the back pages. You sound like a frustrated old man who never made a success, an eight-ulcer man on a four-ulcer job and all four ulcers working.

There are other, more subtle ways:

> For those who like this kind of book, this is the kind of book they will like.
> > —Abraham Lincoln

> He wasn't exactly hostile to facts, but he was apathetic about them.
> > —Wolcott Gibbs of Alexander Woollcott

Then there is the device of noting the inconsequential:

> He's the greatest man who ever came out of Plymouth, Vermont.
> > —Clarence Darrow, on the qualifications of Calvin Coolidge

> I rose by sheer military ability to the rank of Corporal.
> > —Thornton Wilder

> Julia Child is the only person who can explain a glass of water.
> > —Wayland Flowers

Or this, from a campaign appraisal in *The New York Times*:

> . . . no one who knows Mr. Ford's long, dreary record in the House, 25 years of plodding through backdown, would ever accuse him of being a leader. One can paraphrase Winston Churchill's description of Neville Chamberlain—"He would make a good mayor of Grand Rapids—in a quiet year."

And with more sarcasm:

> He graduated from nursery school with blazing honors.

> Wagner's music is better than it sounds.
> > —Mark Twain

Calvin Coolidge done nothin' as president, but it wasn't that he done nothin' that made him a hero—he done it better than anybody.

—Will Rogers

His books did not balance, but his heart always beat warmly for his native land.

—Eulogy for a Texas legislator

Sometimes you may add a bit of ambiguity:

One can't judge Wagner's opera *Lohengrin* after a first hearing. I certainly don't intend hearing it a second time.

—Gioacchino Rossini

Just asking a question is often enough:

It's clever, but is it art?

—Rudyard Kipling

Or faint criticism:

Good furniture pictures, unworthy of praise, and undeserving of blame.

—John Ruskin

Of the German Kaiser:

He is an infernal scoundrel, but that is his only fault.

—James M. Barrie

Of a one-man show:

There was one too many in the cast.

Of a play by Maeterlinck, Tallulah Bankhead said:

There is less in this than meets the eye.

The minimizing metaphor (praising the opposite) is similar in effect:

Sculpture: mud pies which endure.

—Cyril Connolly

Or the reverse:

> A weed is no more than a flower in disguise.
>
> —James Russell Lowell

You'll find that praising failings has much potential:

> This woman resembles the Venus de Milo in many ways. Like her she is extraordinarily old, has no teeth, and has white spots in the yellow surface of her body.
>
> —Heinrich Heine

> Your manuscript is both good and original; but the part that is good is not original, and the part that is original is not good.
>
> —Samuel Johnson

> Bernard Shaw hasn't an enemy in the world—and none of his friends like him.
>
> —Oscar Wilde

> He is a great unrecognized incapacity.
>
> —Carl Otto, Prince von Bismarck, of Napoleon

> If what you don't know can't hurt you, he is absolutely hurt-proof.

Another powerful technique is to use a negative affirmatively. Witness this advertisement for *U.S. News and World Report*:

> Have you ever met anybody who actually reads this magazine?

It continues:

> Only 8 million very, very selective people do read it.
> Because this magazine contains no cute pictures.
> No cute writing.
> No gossip.
> No entertainment.
> No stylishly warmed up old news.
> None. Ever. This magazine isn't pretty.

Does that mean it's designed to repel non-serious readers?
Definitely.
For amusement, you simply have to go elsewhere.
We spare our readers unimportant news.
We spare our advertisers unimportant readers.

Sometimes you can *praise* with faint praise, with a kind of ironic understatement. Ethel Merman once said of Mary Martin:

Mary Martin is okay, if you happen to like talent.

SARCASM

The ultimate in negative "praise" is sarcasm, the device of saying the direct opposite of what you mean. It is usually vicious, caustic, antagonistic, and contains some irony. The Greek term was *sarcasmus* which is translated as "to tear flesh, gnash teeth." The Roman expression was *amara irrisio*, translated "bitter laughing at" or *exacerbatio*, "harshness." And Puttenham called it *bitter taunt*.

It was one of those plays in which all of the actors unfortunately enunciated very clearly.
—Robert Benchley

The scenery was beautiful, but the actors got in front of it. The play left a taste of lukewarm parsnip juice.
—Alexander Woollcott

The English may not like music, but they absolutely love the noise it makes.
—Sir Thomas Beecham

I made it a rule never to smoke while asleep, never to stop smoking while awake and never to smoke more than one cigar at a time.
—Mark Twain at seventy

The difference between wrestling and dancing, I have discovered, is that some holds are barred in wrestling.

—Earl Wilson

When you are down and out, something always turns up—and it is usually the noses of your friends.

—Orson Welles

A "good" family, it seems, is one that used to be better.

—Cleveland Amory

I don't care what is written about me so long as it isn't true.

—Katharine Hepburn

Research is something that tells you that a jackass has two ears.

—Albert D. Lasker

I have found the best way to give advice to your children is to find out what they want and then advise them to do it.

—Harry S Truman

Poverty is a wonderful thing. It sticks to a man after all his friends have forsaken him.

There's another advantage in being poor. The doctor will cure you faster.

—Elbert Hubbard

You can't expect a boy to be depraved until he has been to a good school.

—Saki (H. H. Munro)

EXCUSES, EXCUSES

A well-worn method of excusing yourself is to transfer responsibility, that is, to pass the buck. G. Gordon Liddy, one of those who served time in connection with Watergate, gave a familiar shrug-off. Interviewed after being freed from prison, he is quoted as saying:

> When the prince approaches the lieutenant, the proper response of the lieutenant is *Fiat voluntas tua* [Thy will be done].

Dichologia, also called *anangeon* ("excuse"), is the device of defending an act or speech with excuses—as the result of necessity or by the justice of the cause. Henry Peacham gives as an example:

> I forsook my friend, but the laws compelled me. I kept friendship most faithfully as long as the laws permitted me, and now I am not cast off by will, but by force of law.

> I would remind you that extremism in the defense of liberty is no vice.
> —Barry M. Goldwater accepting
> Republican presidential nomination in
> San Francisco, July 16, 1964

> If I cannot retain my moral influence over a man except by occasionally knocking him down, if that is the only basis upon which he will respect me, then for the sake of his soul I have got occasionally to knock him down.
> —Woodrow Wilson

GIVING REASONS

Giving a reason was *aetiologia* in Greek, *redditio causae* in Latin. It is the basic way to justify an argument or make a point. A famous comment is:

> I have found it impossible to carry the heavy burden of responsibility and to discharge my duties as King as I would wish to do, without the help and support of the woman I love.
> —Edward VIII (later the Duke of Windsor) in his
> farewell address, 1936

SMALL EXCUSES OR NONE AT ALL

A quibbling excuse, especially for saving feelings or reputation, is a well-worn device you can use for avoiding comment:

> The work was killing me; they called me out of bed all hours of the night to receive resignations of prime ministers.
>
> —Vincent Auriol, retiring as President of France, 1954

> Every government has spies in every other country, and every other country knows about them. It is merely a form of international courtesy, like exchange professors. In fact, they give a rather nice cosmopolitan air to the streets.
>
> —Robert Benchley

> I'm leaving because the weather is too good. I hate London when it's not raining.
>
> —Groucho Marx

Nonsaying may be a better way than gainsaying when you feel a need to be modest or when you are discussing a delicate subject. This technique—which the Romans called *occupatio* and the Greeks called *paralepsis*, meaning "disregard"—emphasizes a point by seeming to pass over it:

> I will not tell you that Dr. Johns is the greatest authority in his field, because you already know this.

For another type of situation:

> Only men who compare themselves with God would dare to pretend in this anguished and bloody era that they know the exact road to the promised land.
>
> —Adlai Stevenson

> Senator Taft is the greatest living authority on what General Eisenhower thinks.
>
> —Adlai Stevenson

BECOMING SILENT

Becoming silent, that is, breaking off in the middle of a thought and leaving it incomplete, was called by the Greeks *aposiopesis* and by the Romans *reticentia* ("silence"); Puttenham simply called it *silence*. Your silence is the result of your seeming inability to go on. It can be very dramatic, and it leaves the audience to infer what the rest of your thought is: "He is stupid, lazy, unreliable—but why go on?"

Another indirect approach is making a positive statement in a negative form. The Greeks called this *antenantiosis*.

In a recent Midwestern congressional election campaign where the incumbent woman candidate had been divorced and had remarried, the opponent made his point by such "nonmentions." By frequently insisting that he would not make "the tragedy of divorce" a campaign issue, he did. And his campaign literature made frequent mention of his wife, four daughters, and his role as a "young family man."

Another way of not-saying is the technique of a candidate as reported in *The New York Times*:

> I do not charge outright that Cuomo is a gentleman. Without more evidence than I have at present, this would be an irresponsible smear. I simply point out that he has that look. Nor do I charge that Koch is a gentleman, despite a certain look of pain you catch now and then when Cuomo is accusing him of "pandering" for votes. Nor do I suggest that Koch's look of pain results from guilty suspicion that he really has been "pandering."

And for denying you are making the statement you are really making, there is the classic speech of Mark Antony in *Julius Caesar*:

> Friends, Romans, countrymen, lend me your ears;
> I come to bury Caesar, not to praise him.

Of course, what he goes on to do is nothing *but* praise Caesar.

Gilbert and Sullivan used the device in *The Mikado* in the duet of Yum-Yum and Nanki-Poo: *Nanki-Poo*: Were you not to Ko-Ko plighted . . . I would kiss you fondly thus—(kissing her) . . .

Still another method of indirection or denial of the contrary is used by Ross Munro. Asked to leave China after writing a series of articles, he commented:

Communist countries never expel correspondents for telling lies.

Or in an editorial in *Media Information Newsletter*:

People have accused me of understanding Marshall McLuhan. I would like to plead guilty to this accusation and throw myself upon the mercy of the court, but I don't think I have read more than 200 or 250 of the thousands of pages he has written. I never read *Understanding Media* from cover to cover, yet no book has ever affected my thinking more deeply or given me such a rewarding understanding of my own approach to my work. Before McLuhan I thought I was doing things right but in a peculiar way I just wasn't aware of why. McLuhan taught me that.

Arno Press advertises:

We are not the University of Arno.

AMBIGUITY

Ambiguity is a powerful device for avoiding making a direct statement. Your ambiguous statement is one that can be understood in more than one way or one that is deliberately obscure. Noteworthy among the numerous forms your ambiguity might take are the following:

1. Innuendo—hinting at something.
2. *Enigma* (from the Greek meaning "obscure speech")—a riddle; the answer must be deciphered.
3. Circuitous speech (Greek *schematismus,* meaning "configuration")—not coming directly to the point.
4. Double entendre—double meaning that arises from the fact

that certain words can have more than one interpretation.
5. Grammatical ambiguity—a sentence that can have more than one meaning depending on the punctuation or emphasis on different words.

INNUENDO

The Greeks had a term, *syllogismus*, meaning "hinting at something." The Romans called it *significatio* for "sign." In this device you imply more than you say.

Gerald Ford played football too long without a helmet.
—Lyndon B. Johnson

He is a self-made man and worships his creator.
—John Bright, of Disraeli

Jack Benny played Mendelssohn last night. Mendelssohn lost.

When Mr. Wilbur calls his play *Halfway to Hell*, he underestimates the distance.
—Brooks Atkinson

They say kings are made in the image of God. I feel sorry for God if that is what He looks like.
—Frederick the Great

The covers of this book are too far apart.
—Ambrose Bierce

On an advertising billboard:

Nobody ever started a trend in Cleveland.
—*New York Magazine*

or:

There may be places where Grand Marnier isn't offered after dinner.

ENIGMA

For the Greeks *enigma* was "obscure speech." Sometimes they referred to it as *noema*, "an idea." Puttenham gave it the name *close conceit*. The first response to it is: "Now what do you mean by that?"

> I being a gentleman cannot dictate what I think of you. My secretary being a lady cannot type it. You being neither will understand exactly what I mean.
>
> —L. Lawrence

Hamlet's response to the king's "How fares our cousin Hamlet?":

> Excellent, i' faith; of the chameleon's dish;
> I eat the air, promise crammed; you cannot
> feed capons so.

CIRCUITOUS SPEECH

Circuitous speech was called *schematismos* by the Greeks, meaning "configuration." Thus we have Hamlet pledging Horatio to secrecy:

> Here, as before, never, so help you mercy
> How strange or odd soe'er I bear myself,—
> As I perchance hereafter shall think meet
> To put an antic disposition on—
> That you, at such time seeing me, never shall,
> With arms encumb'red thus, or this headshake,
> Or by pronouncing of some doubtful phrase,
> As, "Well, well, we know," or "We could, an if we would,"
> Or "If we list to speak," or "There be, an if they might."
> Or such ambiguous giving out, to note
> That you know aught of me, —this not to do,
> So grace and mercy at your most need help you,
> Swear.

DOUBLE ENTENDRE

Double entendre—an expression that carries two meanings at the same time—is a test of the writer's skill. Sometimes, of course, the second meaning is unintended:

> These are fine novels of yours; they are invaluable to me. When I come home tired and take up one of them I fall asleep directly.
> —Comment of a faithful servant of Sir Walter Scott's

> A generous gentleman had donated a new loudspeaker to his church in fond memory of his wife.

> Author: Have you read my last book?
> Critic: I hope so.
> —Groucho Marx

> Senators who have no secretaries of their own may take advantage of the girls in the steno pool.
> —Suggested bulletin for senators

Benjamin Disraeli evolved a standard reply to would-be authors who sent him little masterpieces:

> Many thanks: I shall lose no time in reading it.

Another, anticlimactic, version of intentional double entendre:

> From the moment I picked up your book until I laid it down I was convulsed with laughter. Someday I intend reading it.
> —Groucho Marx, referring to S. J. Perelman's *Dawn Ginsbergh's Revenge*

In contemporary advertising the device of double entendre also has its use:

> There is just one word for beer and you know it.
> —Schlitz

Take a tender young thing home for dinner.

—Perdue chickens

All my men wear English Leather.
Or they wear nothing at all.

I never use a deodorant.
Yes I know.

Does she or doesn't she?

—Clairol, Inc.

Stretch pants—the garment that made skiing a spectator sport.

—*Time,* on ski fashions

Give your friends gifts they'll never stop opening.

—Waldenbooks

And under a photo of a front-to-front collision:

Our business-vehicle insurance helps when you meet the competition head on!

—Nationwide Insurance

A recent commentary:

The trouble with the publishing business is that too many people who half a mind to write a book do so.

GRAMMATICAL AMBIGUITY

Grammatical double meaning, termed *amphibologia,* from the Greek meaning "ambiguity," uses grammatical structure to create the equivocal meaning.

In Shakespeare's *Othello,* we find an example:

Cassio: Dost thou hear, my honest friend?
Clown: No, I hear not your honest friend; I hear you.

There are, of course, the famed punctuation problems:

> The teacher says the principal is a dolt.
> The teacher, says the principal, is a dolt.

DIGRESSION

Evading an issue by digression or parrying was called *apoplanesis* by the Greeks.

> I'm for each and against none.
>
> —Dwight D. Eisenhower

> I believe in the forgiveness of sin and the redemption of ignorance.
>
> —Adlai Stevenson, reply to request of heckler for his belief

PLEASANT NONSENSE

You may use pleasant nonsense as another means of avoiding an issue—*graciosa nugatio,* the Romans called it; the Greeks called it *charientismus,* "graceful jest."

> They say I am a captive of the city bosses, of the CIO, and then of the Dixiecrats . . . and then of Wall Street, and then of an organization called ADA. Next week I'll probably read in the papers that I am the captive of a girl Ada. I have not met her yet. I had no idea I was so popular, and I hope I can bear this multiple courtship and captivity with becoming modesty.
>
> —Adlai Stevenson

> I am going to introduce a resolution to have the Postmaster General stop reading books and deliver the mail.
>
> —Senator Gale McGee

> Tired of getting junk mail from someone you don't know? Try getting junk mail from someone you do know.
>
> —Surprise Club

We don't seem to be able to check crime, so why not legalize it and then tax it out of business.

IRRELEVANCIES

The same end, of avoiding an issue, is accomplished when you emphasize the irrelevant to distract attention from a point. The Greeks called this method *heterogenium*, meaning "of a different kind." A Roman device that has a similar effect was called *petitio principii*, or "begging the question," in which the premise and the conclusion really say the same thing. (Begging the question is a logical fallacy.) Here are some examples of irrelevancies, most of them used ironically:

Look at the Swiss! They have enjoyed peace for centuries, and what have they produced? The cuckoo clock!
—Winston Churchill, 1930

How can you expect to govern a country that has 246 kinds of cheese?
—Charles de Gaulle

War is rude and impolite, it quite upsets a nation. It's made of several weeks of fight and years of conversation.
—Comment from the early 1900s

It is now proved beyond doubt that smoking is one of the leading causes of statistics.

If I'd known how much packing I'd have to do I'd have run again.
—Harry S Truman on leaving the White House

In the Middle West, the high school is the place where the band practices.
—Robert M. Hutchins

We did get something—a gift. It was a little cocker spaniel dog in a crate . . . sent all the way from Texas. Black and white and spotted. And our little girl Tricia, the six year old, named it Checkers. And you know the kids love that dog and I just want to say this right now, that regardless of what they say about it, we're going to keep it.

> —Richard M. Nixon, in response to an accusation that he accepted gifts while in office

If I had known there was no Latin word for tea, I would have let the vulgar stuff alone.

> —Hilaire Belloc

Note the following from *Media Industry Newsletter*:

HOW TO AVOID TANGLE WITH FTC: MAKE AD "FUNNY." At 10th Anniversary Seminar of Media Decisions, Margery Waxman Smith, acting director of its bureau of consumer protection of Federal Trade Commission, said FTC will be pursuing two guidelines: increase efficiency of FTC by pursuing those cases that involve greatest number of people, greatest market costs; increase amount of information in marketplace. MIN asked Smith how FTC would substantiate claims made in ad such as "Please don't squeeze the Charmin" since (1) there is no Mr. Whipple; (2) no one goes around squeezing Charmin in supermarket, therefore ad deceptive at least on surface level; (3) what's not being said in ad, according to FTC's guidelines, may be most compelling reason to buy; (4) ad fails to increase amount of product information in marketplace. Smith replied, "It's funny. The Charmin ad is so entertaining. We wouldn't pursue an inquiry into that kind of advertisement."

MORAL OF STORY FOR MARKETERS: Don't make product claims. Learn what advertising messages potential users of your product will resonate with and make the discovery that there's rarely need to make a product claim . . . and besides selling millions of packages, one will never have problem with FTC.

PASSING OVER AN ISSUE

If you want to avoid an issue but do not want to seem to ignore it altogether, you can pass over it very quickly. This was called *metastasis* ("removal" or "change") in Greek, and *transmotio* ("transporting") in Latin. Puttenham called it *remove,* or *flitting figure.* Winston Churchill once responded to a reporter's question by saying:

I think "No comment" is a splendid expression. I am using it again and again. I got it from Sumner Welles.

As a general rule, I abstain from reading the reports of attacks upon myself, wishing not to be provoked by that to which I cannot properly offer an answer.

—Abraham Lincoln, 1865

PARODY AND SATIRE

The technique of parody is based on imitation and mimicry combined with exaggeration of faults, weaknesses, or affectations. It may involve a variety of rhetorical devices, but all utilize the negative approach, that is, a form of criticism is implied. In parody you mock a work of literature or other writing by imitating its form in an exaggerated way. In satire, on the other hand, you provoke mockery or contempt by making the subject matter itself ridiculous. In parody you criticize form; in satire you criticize material. Of course, the two are often combined.

This is a recent bit of parody on the saccharine treatment of the rich working girl as it appears in certain publications:

From the stepmother of a cleaning woman at Viking Press, I have learned that Jackie likes to dial the telephone clockwise, often with one of her fingers. Even more important, she has a marvelously classy way of operating the Xerox machine, for copying anything goes against her grain. "She's terribly real when she's Xeroxing," the stepmother said to me. "And she can do it just as well even without any jewelry."

—*Signature,* October 1976

And a different approach:

One Democratic automobile, the Hubert, designed as the plain people's car, known as the Folks Wagon, has been withdrawn from the race, which is a pity, for it had acceleration. From a standing start, it could roar up to 300 words a minute in five seconds.

—Kenneth Keating

IRONY

Irony, saying the direct opposite of what you intend, is the wit of feigned ignorance and is most effective in a longer monologue where the issue can be hit again and again. The Greeks called it *eironeia* or *enantiosis* ("opposition"). In Latin there are several terms: *dissimulatio* ("concealment") and *illusio* ("mocking") were used most often. Puttenham gave it the name *drie mock.*

Your wit will be more pointed when you make it seem to be unintentional—a dry and seemingly serious statement that requires a second thought on the part of your listener. The force of irony depends on a simple principle: contrast between appearance and reality, incongruity.

Books have to be read. It is the only way of discovering what they contain. A few savage tribes eat them, but reading is the only method of assimilation revealed to the West.

—E. M. Forster

It's very easy to give up smoking; I've done it a thousand times.

—Mark Twain, in his lectures

Bob Hope says: "I've found the secret of youth—I lie about my age."

—Joey Adams

Irony should, in general, be sufficiently obvious so that your reader or listener won't misunderstand, yet not so wounding that it cannot provoke some laughter.

Cited as one of the most effective ironies in English prose is Jonathan Swift's *A Modest Proposal for Preventing the Children of Poor People of Ireland from Being a Burden to Their Parents or Country and Making Them Beneficial to the Public.* It proposes to solve the problem of a starving Irish population by suggesting that the babies born, seen as an excess population, should be treated as animals, slaughtered, and eaten. The monologue goes into great detail as to the best age—one year, at which time they would be most tender, with an alternate age of twelve or thirteen, when they could substitute for venison. Detail is piled on detail. The author recognizes that "it is not improbable that some scrupulous people might be apt to censure such a practice (although indeed very injustly) as a little bordering on cruelty; which I confess, has always been with me the strongest objection against my project, how well soever intended." With straight face the author lists the advantages of his proposal, explains the cooking and serving, the salvaging of the skin for gloves, the method of slaughtering, etc. He then proposes other less drastic remedies—basic reforms, taxing absentee property-owners, the regulation of imports, etc.—and dismisses them as impractical.

Here is a passage from *A Modest Proposal*:

This would be a great inducement to marriage, which all wise nations have either encouraged by rewards, or enforced by laws and penalties. It would increase the care and tenderness of mothers toward their children, when they are sure of a settlement for life, to the poor babes, provided in some sort by the public for their annual profit instead of expense. We should see an honest emulation among the married women, which of them could bring the fattest child to the market, men would become as fond of their wives during the time of their pregnancy, as they are now of their mares in foal, their cows in calf, or sows when they are ready to farrow, nor offer to beat or kick them (as is too frequent a practice) for fear of a miscarriage.

Two classic examples come from *Hamlet*. Commenting on the short period between his father's death and his mother's remarriage, Hamlet says:

> Thrift, thrift, Horatio! the funeral baked meats
> Did coldly furnish forth the marriage tables.

And speaking to Ophelia, who has corrected him, noting that it has been two months, not two hours since his father's death:

So long? . . . O heavens! die two months ago, and not forgotten yet? Then there's hope a great man's memory may outlive his life half a year.

In jokes, irony is less biting:

It's hard to detect good luck—it looks so much like something you've earned.
> —Frank A. Clark, Register & Tribune Syndicate

Sooner or later, a grandparent begins to wonder why babies are entrusted to young people.
> —Harry Karrs

I think housework is the reason most women go to the office.
> —Heloise Cruse

The thing that impresses me most about America is the way parents obey their children.
> —Edward, Duke of Windsor, 1957

NOT TO THE POINT

Circumlocution, from the Latin "to speak around," is also known as *periphrasis* in the Greek; the Romans called it *circuitio* ("going around"), and Puttenham called it *ambage*. For periphrasis you utilize the long word, the metaphor, or descriptive expressions where a short word or phrase could do as well or better. Here is an effective means of obfuscation, avoidance, and euphemism. Periphrasis is acceptable as a storyteller's device: It is part of the element of suspense. The Bible has much of it, and Homer, Virgil, and many writers in the sixteenth through the eighteenth centuries used it in their ornamented, aureate style. It was frequently used by Victorian writers as well. Dickens, for example, wrote: "But an addition to the little party now made its appearance" for "another person came in."

Euphuism, or excessive verbiage by use of figures of speech, is generally a fault in writing. It is an exaggerated circumlocution. You can, however, use it to distract, confuse, equivocate, or avoid an issue.

Euphuism suffuses the text with balanced structures, antitheses, paradoxes, puns and sound plays, patterns of single words, and similes. With this device your word tricks and ornaments drown the meanings. It is virtually a parody of all rhetorical devices.

The Greeks called it *asiatismus* ("a style used by the Asians"), described as full of figures and words but lacking in matter.

The style is named for *Euphues,* a prose romance created by John Lyly in 1580. The two-part book has one section called "The Anatomy of Wit." It is considered a manual of courtly culture, a book of courtesy written in an elegant and artful style that resulted in the term "euphuistic." Lyly became the most popular writer among the English gentry for a while. The popularity was short-lived, however. As less-talented writers adopted the style, the public turned to other fashions in writing. By 1590 it was passé.

Here is Euphues's response to a warning involving the word "nature":

Now whereas you seem to love my nature, and loathe my nurture, you betray your own weakness, in thinking that nature may

anyways be altered by education, and as you gave ensamples to confirm your pretence, so I have most evident and infallible arguments to serve for my purpose:
It is natural for the vine to spread.

In modern times euphuism is considered in bad taste—like the overornamentation of all works of art. But you'll find it has its use as a means of calling attention to something, or of diverting attention from something else.

The Greeks called overlong or bombastic speech *bomphiologia,* meaning "buzzing words," *macrologia* meaning "speaking at length," or *homiologia,* meaning "long-winded speech." Puttenham had a term, *long language.* All these terms describe similar patterns.

This device was a favorite of John L. Lewis. Here he comments on the Taft-Hartley Law in 1954:

Every day I have a matutinal indisposition that emanates from the nauseous effluvia of that oppressive slave statute.

Gladstone once finished a long speech attacking the policies of Disraeli. Disraeli's reply was:

The man needs no reply. He is inebriated by the exuberance of his own verbosity.

Sententiousness, pompous speech, usually with many maxims, is a variation. Oliver Goldsmith described it as "the pompous train, the swelling phrase, the unnatural rant."

I'm not the greatest; I'm the double greatest. Not only do I knock 'em out, I pick the round.
—Muhammad Ali

VIII

FIGURES OF PERSUASION

A PRIMARY OBJECTIVE OF RHETORIC IS PERSUASION. RHET-
oric carries the day in a court of law, changes the views of
legislators who rule the nation, moves the populace to bestow
honor or to declare war. Indeed, since man has listened to
other men, there have been priests and medicine men, dis-
puters and lawmakers, salesmen and diplomats, whose tools
are words. The alternatives to using words have usually been
most unpleasant.

As we have seen, the techniques of persuasion were well
developed even before Cicero, although the critics deplored
its devices to the point of construing rhetoric as a threat to
truth and justice. Soon the same techniques made their way
into everyday prose. The devices you may choose from today
are legion.

WORDS OF ADVICE

The simplest technique of argumentation is simply to give
advice from a position of authority. You may be trying to
dissuade (known to the Romans as *dehortatio*), or just to give
positive advice, or a command to the contrary. Your statement may be brief:

Advice to persons about to marry—Don't.

—*Punch,* 1845

Don't give up the ship!

—James Lawrence

Or lengthy:

What are desirable qualifications for any young man who wishes to become a politician? It is the ability to foretell what is going to happen tomorrow, next week, next month, and next year. (Long pause) And to have the ability afterwards to explain why it didn't happen.

—Winston Churchill

The device of recommending useful precepts is widely used. The Greeks called it *diatyposis* (meaning "vivid description"), the Romans, *testamentum*, meaning "something acknowledged before witnesses." Neither term is used in a literal sense.

If a man is vain, flatter, if timid, flatter, if boastful, flatter. In all history, too much flattery never lost a gentleman.

—Katheryn Cravens

Do the day's work. If it be to protest the rights of the weak, whoever objects, do it. If it be to help a powerful corporation better to serve the people, do that. Expect to be called a demagogue, but don't be a demagogue. Don't hesitate to be as reactionary as the multiplication table. Don't expect to build up the weak by pulling down the strong.

—Calvin Coolidge

If you give your son only one gift, let it be enthusiasm.

—Bruce Barton

If you your lips would keep from slips,
    Five things observe with care;
To whom you speak, of whom you speak,
    And how, and when, and where.

—W. E. Norris

And there is Polonius's advice to Laertes:

> Neither a borrower, nor a lender be;
> For loan oft loses both itself and friend,
> And borrowing dulls the edge of husbandry.
> This above all: to thine own self be true,
> And it must follow, as the night the day,
> Thou canst not then be false to any man.

ANTICIPATING OR ANSWERING AN OBJECTION

Preventing an objection by anticipating it was called variously *procatalepsis* (Greek for "anticipation"), *praeoccupatio* ("concerned in advance"), *praeceptio* ("to receive in advance"), *praesumptio* ("to take for granted"), *ante occupatio* ("before employment"), *anticipatio*, and *prolepsis* ("preconception"), and by Puttenham, *presumptuous*. One example quoted is from I Corinthians 15:35–37:

> But some man will say, How are the dead raised up? and with what body do they come? Thou fool, that which thou sowest is not quickened, except it die: And that which thou sowest, thou sowest not that body that shall be, but bare grain, it may chance of wheat, or of some other grain.

This type of approach, sometimes called the preemptive attack, was used by Zbigniew Brzezinski, President Carter's national security adviser:

> "If you don't agree with us," they are saying, "we're going to stamp you an anti-Semite."

Here is a different approach:

> They accuse me of speaking, when I was abroad, about the injustices to the negro in America. I certainly did.
> —Paul Robeson

An advertiser uses the device in this way:

> If you think the longer it takes to make dentures, the better they'll fit . . . try our same-day service on for size.
>
> —The Denture Center

Turning an opponent's argument to your own use is known as *peristrophe,* from the Greek "turning around."

> The fact that Carter thinks about it but doesn't do anything just goes to show he isn't a man of action.
>
> —About candidate Jimmy Carter's statement in a *Playboy* interview

> Most of the money given by rich people in "charity" is made up of conscience money, "ransom," political bribery, and bids for titles. . . . One buys moral credit by signing a check, which is easier than turning a prayer wheel.
>
> —George Bernard Shaw

The same term is applied to a retort that returns an accusation or an insult. A Congressional doorkeeper tells this story in a popular exposé:

> The story goes that the Speaker was sitting in the House floor library, reading a Cincinnati newspaper from back home when a brash Congressman thought he'd make a splash by putting down Longworth on his womanizing.
>
> "Mr. Speaker," he said, "your pretty bald head reminds me of my wife's behind. Is it all right if I rub my hand across it? Then I'll be sure."
>
> Without waiting for an answer, he went ahead and rubbed his hand all the way across Longworth's bald head and said, "Yes, it does feel just like my wife's behind." He looked around a bit smugly and waited for Longworth to explode. But he didn't. Longworth lifted his own hand and ran it across his own head thoughtfully. "I'll be damned if it doesn't," he said.
>
> —William Fishbait Miller, as told to Frances Speitz Leighton

USING OPPOSITES

Deducing the truth from the assumed truth of the contrary was *enantiosis* (meaning "opposition") to the Greeks, *contrarium* (Latin for "going forward") to the Romans.

If it be great praise to please good men, surely to please evil men is a great shame.

Wouldst thou both eat thy cake and have it?

—Alan Patrick Herbert

Rhetorica ad Herennium IV, xviii cites:

How should you expect one who has ever been hostile to his own interests to be friendly to another's?

War and peace invite the use of the device:

To be prepared for war is one of the most effectual means of preserving peace.

—George Washington

We shall more certainly preserve peace when it is well understood we are prepared for war.

—Andrew Jackson

We are going to have peace even if we have to fight for it.

—Dwight D. Eisenhower, 1948

Expressing doubt—real or feigned—about a point, was called by the Greeks *aporia* (or "being at a loss"), by the Romans, *dubitatio* ("wavering in opinion"), and by Puttenham *doubtful*:

Whether he took them from his fellows more impudently, gave them to a harlot more lasciviously, removed them from the Roman people more wickedly or altered them more presumptuously, I cannot well declare.

—Cicero

If he [the candidate] purported to know the answer to everything, he would be either a knave or a fool. . . . And finally, if he should arrive at election time with almost everybody satisfied, then you should, by all means, vote against him as the most dangerous charlatan of them all.

—Adlai Stevenson

Don't tell me of facts, I never believe facts; you know Canning said nothing was so fallacious as facts, except figures.

—Sydney Smith

I come from a state that raises corn and cotton and cockleburs and Democrats, and frothy eloquence neither convinces nor satisfies me. I am from Missouri. You have got to show me.

—William D. Vandiver

MOCKING

Mocking an opponent's speech, gestures, or habits by exaggeration—the Greek word was *hypocrisis* (meaning "reply")—is still effective today:

Too often Washington's reflex is to discover a problem and then throw money at it, hoping it will somehow go away.

—Kenneth B. Keating

The real question is whether a platform represents the clicking of a ghost's typewriter, if I may put it that way, or the beating of a human heart.

—Adlai Stevenson

DISPARAGING AN ARGUMENT

Disparagement of your opponent's argument is, of course, routine in any debate. The Greeks called it *diasyrmus,* meaning "disparagement," the Romans, *elevatio,* meaning "lessening." It is a mild, almost chiding device.

You may prove anything by figures.

—Quoted by Carlyle

. . . it was the triumph of hope over experience.

—Boswell, quoting Samuel Johnson's remark referring to the second marriage of a friend

POINTING OUT

Inter se pugnantia (from the Latin meaning "fighting between themselves") is the device of pointing out inconsistencies or hypocrisies in your antagonist. Thus Henry Peacham offers an example from Romans 2:21–24:

Thou therefore which teachest another teachest thou not thyself? thou that preachest a man should not steal, dost thou steal? Thou that sayest a man shall not commit adultery, dost thou commit adultery? thou that abhorrest idols, dost thou commit sacrilege? Thou that makest thy boast of the law, through breaking the law dishonourest thou God? For the name of God is blasphemed among the Gentiles through you, as it is written.

You don't set a fox to watching the chickens just because he has a lot of experience in the hen house.

—Harry S Truman, on Richard Nixon's candidacy, 1960

There is a counterpart:

Whenever the press quits abusing me, I know I'm in the wrong pew.

—Harry S Truman

I don't want to belong to any club that will accept me as a member.

—Groucho Marx

INVIDIOUS COMPARISON

Then there is the invidious comparisons, a form of *tapinosis* (Greek for "reduction, humiliation"):

The man most sought after as a public servant combines the best qualities of the milkman's horse: he must raise no important problems and he must know where to stop.

—Howard Morgan

When we know as much about people as hog specialists know about hogs, we'll be better off.

—Lewis Hershey

The point about white Burgundies is that I hate them myself . . . so closely resembling a blend of cold chalk soup and alum cordial with an additive or two to bring it to the colour of children's pee.

—Kingsley Amis

There is not one single social or economic principle or concept in the philosophy of the Russian Bolshevik which has not been realized, carried into action, and enshrined in immutable laws a million years ago by the white ant.

—Winston Churchill, 1917

TO THE ABSURD

Reductio ad absurdum—reducing or extending an argument to an absurd ultimate conclusion—is popular in today's usage. Here are some ways in which it is used:

Eventually—eventually we all are dead.

A newspaper reported that I spend $30,000 a year buying Paris clothes and that women hate me for it. I couldn't spend that much unless I wore sable underwear.

—Jacqueline Kennedy

"My advice to you," the mechanic said, "is that you keep the oil and change the car."

Due to lack of interest, tomorrow has been cancelled.

We didn't mind so much that our local postmaster read all our mail, but when he started answering it, we thought he went too far.

—Herb Shriner

It is good to be helpful and kindly, but don't give yourself to be melted into candle grease for the benefit of the tallow trade.

—George Eliot

When everybody is somebody, then nobody is anybody.

Politicians are the same all over. They promise to build a bridge even where there is no river.

—Nikita Khrushchev

We cannot put the face of a person on a stamp unless said person is deceased. My suggestion, therefore, is that you drop dead.

—James Edward Day, Postmaster General,
to a petitioner who wanted himself portrayed
on a postage stamp

REJECTING AN ARGUMENT

When you reject a point as insignificant, wicked, or erroneous you are using *antirrhesis* (Greek for "counterstatement" or "refutation").

The tax which will be paid for the purpose of education is not more than the thousandth part of what will be paid to kings, priests and nobles who will rise up among us if we leave the people in ignorance.

—Thomas Jefferson

Rejecting a point indignantly as impertinent or absurd was called *apodixis*, Greek for "I answer" and, later, *rejectio*, meaning "throwing away," by the Romans. Here are some applications:

If I do not believe as you believe, it proves that you do not believe as I believe, and this is all that it proves.

Bernard Shaw one day received an invitation from a celebrity hunter:

Lady X will be home Thursday between four and six.

The author returned the card; underneath he had written:

Mr. Bernard Shaw likewise.

—*Reader's Digest,* 1939

PREPARATION

The buildup—a gradual preparation for your point—was variously called *procatasceue,* from the Greek "prepare beforehand" or *praeparatio,* from the Latin "preparation."

For want of a nail the shoe was lost; for want of a shoe the horse was lost; and for want of a horse the rider was lost: being overtaken and slain by the enemy, all for want of care about a horseshoe nail.

—Benjamin Franklin

When wicked persons have gone on in a course of sin, and find they have reason to fear the just judgment of God for their sins, they begin at first to wish that there were no God to punish them; then by degrees they persuade themselves that there is none; and then they set themselves to study for arguments to back their opinion.

—John Bunyan

STEP BY STEP

Advancing step by step was called by the Greeks *auxesis* (meaning "amplification"), the Romans *progressio.* It does not necessarily involve a climax.

If you owe $275 you're a piker; if you owe $275 thousand you're a businessman; if you owe $275 million you're a tycoon; and if you owe $275 billion you're the government.

When angry, count ten before you speak; if very angry, a hundred.

—Thomas Jefferson

New opinions often appear first as jokes and fancies, then as blasphemies and treasons, then as questions open to discussion, and finally as established truths.

—George Bernard Shaw

ALTERNATIVES

There are many techniques you may use for persuading with alternatives. The Greeks and Romans classified them principally as:

Alloiosis (Greek for "difference")—the breaking down into alternatives.

Deliberatio (Latin for "reflection")—evaluating possible courses.

Apophasis (Greek for "denial")—providing alternatives and rejecting each.

Antisagoge—offering two or more options.

Expeditio (Latin for "to untangle the feet from a snare") —rejecting all but one of the alternatives.

Dilemma (Greek for "double proposition")—offering unacceptable choices.

Prosapodosis—giving a reason for each course of action.

Contrarium (Latin for "the opposite")—the use of two opposite alternatives, one used to disprove the other.

Developing, accepting, rejecting, and selecting alternatives can be the basis of convincing logical and pseudological persuasion. The process implies an open creative mind bent on finding the best solution.

Thus, the breaking down into alternatives (*alloiosis*):

A kiss can be a comma, a question mark or an exclamation point. That's basic spelling that every woman ought to know.

—Mistinguette

There are three ways of doing something—the right way, the wrong way and the Army way.

Deliberatio—evaluating possible courses:

. . . it is a great deal better that some people should prosper too much than that no one should prosper enough.

—Theodore Roosevelt

An optimist is a person who sees a green light everywhere . . . while the pessimist sees only the red stop light. . . . But the truly wise person is color blind.

—Albert Schweitzer

Analyzing each of the alternatives and rejecting each (*apophasis*):

If I could save the Union, I would save it the shortest way under the Constitution. . . . If I could save the Union without freeing any slave, I would do it; and if I could save it by freeing all the slaves, I would do it. . . . What I do about slavery and the colored race, I do because I believe it helps to save the Union; and what I forbear, I forbear because I do not believe it helps to save the union.

—Abraham Lincoln

There are two periods when Congress does no business: one is before the holidays, and the other is after.

—G. D. Prentice

The only months in which he'd consider getting married are those that have a "w" in them.

Antisagoge, later called *compensatio*, offers two or more options, e.g., do it and . . . or don't do it, with equal emphasis.

One has two duties—to be worried and not to be worried.

—E. M. Forster

Selecting one alternative (*expeditio*) was called *speedie dispatcher* by Puttenham.

An honorable defeat is better than a dishonorable victory.

—Millard Fillmore

A famous actress explains that her husband has always felt that marriage and a career don't mix: So ever since we got married he hasn't worked.

—Earl Wilson

The Union—no North—no South—no East—no West—but a sacred maintenance of the common brotherhood.

—Franklin Pierce

Democracy is the worst form of government except all those other forms that have been tried from time to time.

—Winston Churchill

There is an old saying here that a man must do three things during his life: plant trees, write books and have sons. I wish they would plant more trees and write more books.

—Luis Muñoz Marin, Governor of Puerto Rico

Offering unacceptable choices (*dilemma*, also known as *ceratin*, from the Greek, "made of horn"):

There is only one thing worse than fighting with allies, and that is fighting without them.

—Harry S Truman

She's at that awkward stage—too old to be a Brownie and too young to be a bunny.

—Henny Youngman

I'm too big to cry and it hurts too much to laugh.

—Adlai Stevenson paraphrasing Abraham Lincoln

Supporting each suggestion with a reason, called *prosapo-dosis* or *redditio* ("giving a reason"):

He must either feed her or kill her: feed her if he needs her; let her die if he does not care.

The use of two opposite alternatives, one used to disprove the other (*contrarium*):

I would rather fail in a cause that someday will triumph than to win in a cause that I know someday will fail.

—Woodrow Wilson

The test of our progress is not whether we add more to the abundance of those who have much; it is whether we provide enough for those who have too little.

—Franklin D. Roosevelt

We are here to make a choice between the quick and the dead.

—Bernard M. Baruch

Old age isn't so bad when you consider the alternative.

—Maurice Chevalier

If good men don't hold office, bad men will.

—Calvin Coolidge

The inherent vice of Capitalism is the unequal sharing of blessings. The inherent virtue of Socialism is the equal sharing of miseries.

—Winston Churchill

She's so suspicious, if she finds no blond, black, or red hairs on his jacket, she accuses him of running around with bald women.

If you feel neglected, think of Whistler's father.

Dialysis (Greek for "separation") uses two hypothetical situations (Puttenham called it *dismembrer*):

Either Tom is too old to travel or he is broke.

. . . either wipe out the slum, or it wipes us out.

—Jacob A. Riis

Broadly speaking, any middle-of-the-road politician faces one of two prospects. He can allow himself to be torn in two by the forces he is attempting to conciliate. Or he can draw strength from both irreconcilable extremes by playing one off against the other.

—Samuel Lubell

DENIAL

Denial requires a special skill. Unless you present it effectively, denial may simply perpetuate the false statement you are making—without convincing anyone of its nontruth.

I never did, or countenanced, in public life, a single act inconsistent with the strictest good faith; having never believed there was one code of morality for a public, and another for a private man.

—Thomas Jefferson

Denial can be the best defense if you couch it in terms more elaborate than a simple "I didn't do it." Here are some excellent ones:

When you try to conquer other people or extend yourself over vast areas you cannot win in the long run. . . .

The Russians today foolishly think that we are imperialistic and want to conquer their land. The very opposite is true. They are the imperialists. We are not imperialists. We do not want any more territory. We do not want to conquer any people. We want to help people because helping them means helping ourselves.

—Harry S Truman

I am informed from many quarters that a rumour has been put about that I died this morning. This is quite untrue.

—Winston Churchill, 1951

If Marilyn is in love with my husband it proves she has good taste, for I am in love with him, too.
—Simone Signoret, of rumors linking her husband,
Yves Montand, with actress Marilyn Monroe, 1960

I never said all Democrats were saloon keepers; what I said was all saloon keepers were Democrats.
—Horace Greeley

CHAPTER

FIGURES OF EMOTION AND FALLACY

As MOST OF US HAVE LEARNED, IN THE WORLD OF PERSUAsion logic has its limitations. In everyday situations it is often wiser to woo with sweet words than with ponderous briefs, to appeal to ego rather than to good sense. In the credo of advertising, the greatest effect is reached through an emotional appeal: "Don't sell the steak, sell the sizzle." Rhetoricians, wise through the ages, have left a legacy of devices and techniques as useful today as they were two thousand years ago.

GOD AND COUNTRY

From earliest times, a call to the deity or invoking the deity has been both an excuse and an escape from praise or criticism. *Deesis*, from the Latin for god, and *obtestatio*, "vehement supplication," were the names given to such appeals:

Let us raise a standard to which the wise and honest can repair; the rest is in the hands of God.

—George Washington

All is wisely ordered by Providence.

—John Tyler

No less famous, perhaps, is the latter-day comment of

Chaplain Howell M. Forgy on Pearl Harbor that fateful December 7, 1941:

> Praise the Lord and pass the ammunition.

Grantland Rice coined another famous sentence:

> For when the One Great Scorer comes to write against your name, He marks—not that you won or lost—but how you played the game.

Defending John Brown shortly after the raid on Harpers Ferry, Wendell Phillips declared:

> One on God's side is a majority.

And a later adaptation:

> One, with God, is always a majority, but many a martyr has been burned at the stake while the votes were being counted.
> —Thomas B. Reed

> America is the greatest force that God has ever allowed to exist on His footstool.
> —Dwight D. Eisenhower

Sometimes as effective as an appeal to the deity is a reference to a historical figure:

> If I have erred, I err in the company of Abraham Lincoln.
> —Theodore Roosevelt

Prayer was more commonly used in all phases of life until this generation, but has not been abandoned as a format in public life. The Greeks called it *euche*, which translates as "prayer."

> Build me a son, O Lord, who will be strong enough to know when he is weak, and brave enough to face himself when he is afraid, one who will be proud and unbending in honest defeat, and humble and gentle in victory.
> —General Douglas MacArthur

I pray Heaven to bestow the best of blessings on this house and all that shall hereafter inhabit it. May none but honest and wise men ever rule under this roof.

—John Adams to Abigail Adams (1800)

Before all else, we seek, upon our common labor as a nation, the favor of Almighty God. And the hopes in our hearts fashion the deepest prayers of our people.

May we pursue the right—without self-righteousness

May we know unity—without conformity

May we grow in strength—without pride of self

May we, in our dealings with all people of the earth, ever speak the truth and serve justice.

May the light of freedom, coming to all darkened lands, flame brightly—until at last the darkness is no more.

May the turbulence of our age yield to a true time of peace, when men and nations shall share a life that honors the dignity of earth, the brotherhood of all.

—Dwight D. Eisenhower

My fellow Americans, I once asked for your prayers, and now I give you mine. May God guide this wonderful country, its people, and those they have chosen to lead them. May our third century be illuminated by liberty and blessed with brotherhood, so that we and all who come after us may be the humble servants of thy peace. Amen.

—Gerald Ford

Flag and country also have great power to inspire an emotional response. The moving force is genuine patriotism at some times, but mere chauvinism at others. One way or another, such appeals have a magic never to be denied by rational men who do not want to be accused of treason.

Nathan Hale's words, as he was about to be hanged as a spy on September 22, 1776, remain immortal:

I only regret that I have but one life to lose for my country.

And President Andrew Jackson's toast at a Jefferson's Birthday dinner in Washington, April 13, 1830:

Our federal Union! it must be preserved!

Also memorable are the words of Commodore Stephen Decatur, at a dinner in his honor in 1816, after a triumph over the Barbary pirates.

Our Country! In her intercourse with foreign nations, may she always be in the right; but our country, right or wrong.

Chauvinism may take the form of historic bravado. Ulysses S. Grant wrote from Spotsylvania Court House, Pennsylvania, May 11, 1864:

I propose to fight it out on this line, if it takes all summer.

Many of us recall:

We mean to hold our own. I have not become the King's First Minister in order to preside over the liquidation of the British Empire.

—Winston Churchill

LOOKING BACK

Calling on tradition or the experience of history has been an effective appeal for the writer and speaker. The Greeks called it *anamnesis*, "remembering," the Romans *recordatio*, "recalling to mind."

There is no king who has not had a slave among his ancestors, and no slave who has not had a king among his.

—Helen Keller

From Caesar to Cromwell, and from Cromwell to Napoleon . . . history presents the same solemn warning—beware of elevating to the highest civil trust the commander of your victorious armies.

—James Buchanan

Sometimes it is pure nostalgia:

And what is so rare as a day in June?
—James Russell Lowell, *The Vision of Sir Launfal,*
1848

Lafayette, we are here.
> —Colonel Charles E. Stanton recalling in 1917
> Lafayette's help to the U.S. during the Revolutionary
> War

I didn't realize what my father did for a living until I was six. Then a playmate at school told me. That night when Father came home he flopped down into his easy chair. I approached him with awe. He didn't look famous to me. I asked, "Are you Walt Disney?"

"You know I am," he said.

"The Walt Disney?" I insisted.

He looked startled; then he grinned and nodded. Whereupon I said the five words he must have thought he was safe from in the bosom of his family: "Please give me your autograph."
> —Diane Disney Miller

Four barges into everything
(Hearts, too) without a knock.
Four will be five on the twelfth of July,
And I wish I could stop the clock.
> —Eloise Gibbs, "Four"

. . . I have found out in later years we were very poor, but the glory of America is that we didn't know it then.
> —Dwight D. Eisenhower

If you do climb upon his knee, do it with love and remember he is a great human person, make him happy that the children in this great city of New York want to hold his hand, touch his head and sit on his lap. For here we are today, all these 150 years later, still loving his stories.
> —Eva Le Gallienne, at the Hans
> Christian Andersen statue in
> Central Park

An advertisement pulls the same strings:

You've come a long way, baby.
> —Virginia Slims

CITING AN AUTHORITY

Apomnemonysis (meaning "recounting") was the term used by the Greeks, *commemoratio* (meaning "bring to remembrance") by the Romans, for quoting words of authority. There are several ways in which you can do this:

> One of the wisest things my daddy ever told me was that so-and-so is a damned smart man, but the fool's got no sense.
> —Lyndon B. Johnson

> This is daddy's bedtime secret for today: Man is born broken. He lives by mending. The grace of God is glue.
> —Eugene O'Neill

> They asked Lucan, the fabulist, "From whom did you learn manners?" He answered: "From the unmannerly."
> —Saadi (the Persian poet)

Appealing to historical parallels and citing tradition can be persuasive because it provokes feelings of nostalgia or patriotism in your reader or listener:

> In 1776 the fight was for democracy in taxation. In 1936 that is still the fight. . . . One sure way to determine the social conscience of a government is to examine the way taxes are collected and how they are spent. And one sure way to determine the social conscience of an individual is to get his tax-reaction. Taxes, after all, are the dues that we pay for the privileges of membership in an organized society. . . . Here is my principle: Taxes shall be levied according to ability to pay. That is the only American principle.
> —Franklin D. Roosevelt

> I do not forget that I am a mechanic. I am proud to own it. Neither do I forget that Adam was a tailor, sewing fig leaves together for aprons; Tubal-cain was an artificer in brass and iron; Joseph the husband of Mary was a carpenter, and our Savior probably followed the same trade; the apostle Paul was a

tentmaker; Socrates was a sculptor; Archimedes was a mechanic; King Crispin was a shoemaker; and so was Roger Sherman, who helped to form the Constitution.

—Andrew Jackson

King James loved his old shoes best. Who does not? Indeed these new clothes are often won and worn after a most painful birth. . . . A man who has at length found out something important to do will not have to get a new suit to do it in.

—Henry David Thoreau

My delegation cannot refrain from speaking on this question. We have had such an intimate knowledge of boxcars and of deportations to unknown destinations that we cannot be silent.

—Golda Meir, 1956, on Soviet action in Hungary

The trouble with the Republican Party is that it has not had a new idea for thirty years. I am not speaking as a politician; I am speaking as an historian.

—Woodrow Wilson

The Greeks and Romans defined many more devices. *Argumentum ad baculum*—from the Latin "club"—is an appeal to force to settle the argument:

Millions for defense, but not one cent for tribute.

—Robert Goodloe Harper

. . . if they mean to have a war let it begin here!

—Capt. John Parker at Lexington, 1775

CALLS TO ACTION

A call for action and sacrifice—for home and country, or for any cause—can be highly inspiring, if your plan appears to be unselfish or uplifting. This process requires that you move your audience to great emotion, reflecting your own enthusiasm. The Romans called it *exuscitatio*, which translates as "awakening."

My fellow citizens of the world: ask not what your country can do for you—ask what you can do for your country.
—John F. Kennedy

Be ashamed to die until you have won some victory for humanity.
—Horace Mann

Eternal vigilance by the people is the price of liberty, and . . . you must pay the price if you wish to secure the blessing.
—Andrew Jackson

No man who thinks first of himself, and afterwards of his country can call himself an American. America must be enriched by us. We must not live upon her; she must live by means of us.
—Woodrow Wilson

People of France, great people! Pride! Courage! Hope!
—Charles de Gaulle

WHAT CAN'T BE STOPPED

You'll find that an appeal to the practical or acceptance of the inevitable is often called for:

I believe in the Providence of the most men, the largest purse, and the longest cannon.
—Abraham Lincoln

We must . . . make the best of Mankind as they are, since we cannot have them as we wish.
—George Washington

I shall be able to rest one minute after I die.
—Pius XII, to physicians who asked him to curtail his work

The excitement of any great emotion, such as defiance, now known as stonewalling, was *pathopoeia* (Greek for "excitement of passion"). A vehement challenge to action was called

by the Greeks *proclees*, and by the Romans *provocatio*, both
meaning "challenge."

As long as I count the votes, what are you going to do about it?
—William M. Tweed

If *this* be treason, make the most of it.
—Patrick Henry

I don't meet competition. I crush it.
—Charles Revson

I know not what course others may take, but as for me, give me
liberty or give me death!
—Patrick Henry

The public be damned.
—Cornelius Vanderbilt

PREDICTING

Prophesying evil, in Greek, *cataplexis* ("amazement"), in
Latin, *ominatio*, has ancient roots. There is always a Jeremiah
in the bleachers.

Indeed, I tremble for my country when I reflect that God is just.
—Thomas Jefferson

The country needs to be born again; she is polluted with the lust
of power, the lust of gain.
—Margaret Fuller, 1845

NO FISHING AND NO HUNTING. SURVIVORS WILL BE
PROSECUTED.

One man was so mad at me that he ended his letter: Beware.
You will never get out of this world alive.
—John Steinbeck

The Ship of Democracy, which has weathered all storms, may sink through the mutiny of those on board.

—Grover Cleveland

After I die I shall return to earth as the door-keeper of a bordello and I won't let one of you in.

—Arturo Toscanini, to an orchestra that displeased him

A railroad! It would frighten horses, put the owners of public vehicles out of business, break up inns and taverns and be a monopoly generally.

—Andrew Johnson, 1835

Prophesying prosperity was not in the Greek mode but is common among modern politicians. In a speech on October 22, 1928, Herbert Hoover made the famous remark:

Prosperity is just around the corner.

The tradition continues:

We are nearer today to the ideal of the abolition of poverty and fear from the lives of men and women than ever before in any land.

—Lyndon B. Johnson

Being an optimist or quoting one can draw attention to your ideas:

When any calamity has been suffered, the first thing to be remembered is, how much has been escaped.

—Samuel Johnson

Reflect upon your present blessings, of which every man has many: not on your past misfortunes, of which all men have some.

—Charles Dickens

Had he been captain of the *Titanic* he would have announced on impact: "One moment please, we have just stopped to take on ice."

Or just predicting can make your statement memorable:

. . . in this world nothing is certain but death and taxes.

—Benjamin Franklin

Someday, taking its pattern from the United States, there will be founded a United States of Europe.

—George Washington

Addressing the future is also effective:

Posterity! You will never know how much it costs the present generation to preserve your freedom! I hope you will make good use of it! If you do not, I shall repent it in Heaven that I ever took half the pains to preserve it!

—John Adams to Abigail Adams

An advertising use? Johnnie Walker uses this for Black Label Scotch:

Your horoscope indicates that your hard work is about to be richly rewarded.

PROMISES

Exhorting your listeners by promises or threats to act was called *protrope* (the Greek meaning "exhortation") or *adhortatio* (the Latin meaning "encouragement"). Promises and threats can be a type of prediction:

I pledge you, I pledge myself, to a new deal for the American people.

—Franklin D. Roosevelt, 1932

In executing the duties of my present important station, I can promise nothing but purity of intentions, and in carrying these into effect, fidelity and diligence.

—George Washington

REPROACH

Categoria (Greek for "accusation") is reproaching a person to his face. The Romans called it *accusatio*. A famed example is from Matthew 26:20–21:

> Now when the even was come, he sat down with the twelve, And as they did eat, he said, Verily I say unto you, that one of you shall betray me.

Another kind of reproach or rebuke you may use was called *exprobatio* in Latin; in Greek it is *onedismus*. It accuses your opponent of ingratitude:

> They hired the money, didn't they? Let them pay it.
> —Calvin Coolidge, 1925

Asking fairness or justice is a variation:

> All I ask for the Negro is that if you do not like him, let him alone. If God gave him but little, that little let him enjoy.
> —Abraham Lincoln

> Expedience and justice frequently are not even on speaking terms.
> —Arthur H. Vandenberg

FORGIVENESS AND GRATITUDE

Forgiving was known to the Greeks as *syngnome*, translated as "forbearance." In the West the most famous example is:

> Father, forgive them; for they know not what they do.
> —Luke 23:34

From Heine's memoirs comes:

> Since I myself stand in need of God's pity, I have granted an amnesty to all my enemies.

The Greeks called giving thanks *eucharistia*, "a thanksgiving"; in Latin it is *gratiarum actio*, "giving thanks." It still has a universal appeal.

Let us give thanks—if only for the bad things that are never going to happen.

—Old proverb

If a Jew breaks a leg, he thanks God he did not break both legs; if he breaks both, he thanks God he did not break his neck.

—Yiddish proverb

But sometimes it is mentioned with sarcasm:

Thanksgiving is the only kind of giving some people know.

THE SAD SIDE

Lamentation was *threnos* in Greek, meaning "dirge," and in Latin *lamentatio*. Some recent applications:

Over the hill to the poorhouse I'm trudgin' my weary way.

—Will Carleton

Nobody knows the trouble I've seen . . .

—Negro spiritual

These are the times that try men's souls.

—Thomas Paine, 1776

I have a rendezvous with Death
At some disputed barricade.

—Alan Seeger, 1916, who was killed in
World War I that year

Pathos is the conveyance of an experience of suffering or the stirring of the more violent emotions. (The calmer emotions were called *ethos* by Quintilian.) This appeal to pity is as old as creditors and judges. The Greeks had another word for it, *oictros* ("pitiable"), which means specifically to gain forgiveness by moving to tears.

> To be forsaken by all mankind seems to be the destiny that awaits my last days.
>
> —John Quincy Adams

The inscription on the Statue of Liberty in New York Harbor is a classic:

> Give me your tired, your poor,
> Your huddled masses, yearning to breathe free,
> The wretched refuse of your teeming shore,
> Send these, the homeless, tempest-tossed, to me:
> I lift my lamp beside the golden door.
>
> —Emma Lazarus

Bathos, in one of several definitions, describes an emotional appeal that evokes laughter—whether this was your intention or not!—because it is overdone pathos.

> I love to see other mayors; misery loves company.
>
> —Seattle Mayor Wesley C. Uhlman

PRAISE AND COMPLIMENTS

Encomium—the Greek *eulogia* ("praiser," "blessing"), the Latin *commendatio*—is the presentation of praise.

> The well assured and most enduring memorial to Lincoln is invisibly there, today, tomorrow and for a long time yet to come in the hearts of lovers of Liberty, men and women who understand that wherever there is freedom there have been those who fought, toiled and sacrificed for it.
>
> —Carl Sandburg

> You may not like him, but he meets the test of greatness. He fills the living space around him. He cannot be trespassed upon, or toyed with, or subtracted from. Whatever ground he stands on, it is his.
>
> —Henry Luce, of Douglas MacArthur

God could not be everywhere, so therefore he made mothers.

—Hebrew proverb

At the death of William Morris:

You can lose a man like that by your own death, but not by his.

—George Bernard Shaw

One of your more difficult tasks in writing or speaking is expressing a personal compliment that is original, not too saccharine, and not having the sound of flattery:

Her commanding presence was pure electricity.

This was the noblest Roman of them all.

—William Shakespeare, *Julius Caesar*

I love you twenty-four hours more than I did yesterday.

—*Reader's Digest*

PLEDGING CONSTANCY

Pledging constancy was called *eustathia*, from the Greek "tranquility," and *constantia* by the Romans.

The mails must go through.

—Postal Service slogan

I can die at my post but I cannot desert it.

—Elijah P. Lovejoy, abolitionist editor to a mob attacking his office, 1837 (Lovejoy was killed by a mob four days later.)

My hat's in the ring. The fight is on and I'm stripped to the buff.

—Theodore Roosevelt, 1912

I wish to believe in immortality—I wish to live with you forever.

—John Keats, letter to Fanny Brawne

INVOLVING YOUR AUDIENCE

Involving your audience is always useful. The Greeks used a device they called *anacoenosis*, which translates as "communicate with" or "take counsel with." Puttenham called it *impartener*.

Any government, like any family, can for a year spend a little more than it earns. But you and I know that a continuance of that habit means the poorhouse.

—Franklin D. Roosevelt

I will do my best. That well I can do. I ask your help—and God's.

—Lyndon B. Johnson on assuming office

Toyota uses the device:

You asked for—you got it.

Complimenting your listeners or readers always sits well with an audience. It was called *comprobatio*, the Latin for "approval."

Arguments out of a pretty mouth are unanswerable.

—Joseph Addison

This generation of Americans has a rendezvous with destiny.

—Franklin D. Roosevelt, 1936

I think this is the most extraordinary collection of talent, of human knowledge, that has ever been gathered together at the White House—with the possible exception of when Thomas Jefferson dined alone.

—John F. Kennedy, at a White House dinner for U.S.
winners of the Nobel Prize

PERSONAL PROJECTIONS

A personal statement, projecting your personal emotion, can have great poignancy:

I'm living in a house and I know I built it. I work in a workshop which was constructed by me. I speak a language which I developed. And I know I shape my life according to my desires by my own ability. I feel I am safe, I can defend myself. I am not afraid. This is the greatest happiness a man can feel—that he could be a partner with the Lord in creation. This is the real happiness of man: creative life, conquest of nature, and a great purpose.

—David Ben-Gurion

You feel you are no longer clothing yourself; you are dressing a national monument.

—Eleanor Roosevelt

I have said what I meant and meant what I said. I have not done as well as I should like to have done, but I have done my best, frankly and forthrightly; no man can do more and you are entitled to no less.

—Adlai Stevenson

I think the American public wants a solemn ass as a President and I think I'll go along with them.

—Calvin Coolidge

Humility—real or feigned—especially when seasoned with humor is another effective means of establishing a rapport with your audience.

Pat doesn't have a mink coat. But she does have a respectable Republican cloth coat.

—Senator Richard M. Nixon, 1952

Basic research is what I am doing when I don't know what I am doing.

—Wernher von Braun

It is quite flattering . . . but whenever I feel this way I always remember that if instead of making a political speech I was being hanged, the crowd would be twice as big.

—Winston Churchill in response to a compliment on
crowds who came to hear him

If Russians knew how to read, they would write me off.

—Catherine the Great

How do I work? I grope.

—Albert Einstein

You don't live there [in the White House]. You are only Exhibit A to the Country.

—Theodore Roosevelt

I don't feel like a gift from Providence, and I really don't believe I am. I feel very much like a corn-fed Illinois lawyer who had gotten into the big time unintentionally.

—Adlai Stevenson

And the opposite, unashamed egotism:

I never climbed any ladder. I have achieved eminence by sheer gravitation.

—George Bernard Shaw

L'état c'est moi. [I am the state.]

—Attributed to Louis XIV of France

In those days the Lord President was wiser than he is now; he used frequently to take my advice.

—Winston Churchill

I am the Roman King, and am above grammar.

—Sigismund, at the Council of Constance

Why should I get another man to praise me when I can praise myself? I have no disabilities to plead: produce me your best critic, and I will criticize his head off.

—George Bernard Shaw

Winston Churchill's remark to an interpreter is classic: In Paris in 1919, speaking before French notables, he was advised to have an interpreter read his speech. He heard it delivered with such effect that the interpreter received thunderous applause. Churchill was ignored. But not for long. He stepped forward, and in French remarked:

Until I heard your splendid version, Monsieur, I did not realize what a magnificent, indeed, epoch-making speech I had made. Allow me to embrace you, Monsieur.

And later on his seventy-fifth birthday in 1949, in whimsy:

I am ready to meet my Maker. Whether my Maker is prepared for the great ordeal of meeting me is another matter.

INVECTIVE

The most direct of emotional rhetorical devices you can use is the insult, the invective—the plain cussing of an opponent. Here is one classic of vituperation which has been set to music by Hector Berlioz in *The Damnation of Faust.*

Living next to Beelzebub,
Thou art steeped in the most sinful mire,
Fed on filth since childhood.
Know: thy sabbath thou wilt celebrate without us.
Rotten cancer, Salonica's refuse,
Horrid nightmare that cannot be told
Cock-eyed, rotten and noseless,
Thou wert born when thy mother
Writhed in spasms of filth.
Mad butcher of Padolie, look:
Thou art covered with wounds, cankers and scabs.
Rump of a horse, snout of a pig,
Let all the medicinals be bought
For thou to care for thy ills.

Good taste puts some restraint on the epithets you might choose:

The townspeople are morons, yokels, peasants and genus homo boobiensis . . . surrounded by gaping primates from the upland valleys.

—H. L. Mencken

They share the insult of each other's presence.

—Christopher Isherwood

To build an ethical stone wall around President Nixon at this point would require a Merlin of a stonemason. Father John McLaughlin is merely an apprentice bricklayer with a forked tongue for a trowel and hot air for mortar.

—Newsweek

He is a man of splendid abilities, but utterly corrupt. He shines and stinks like rotten mackerel by moonlight.

—John Randolph (1773–1833), of Edward Livingston

Pearson is an infamous liar, a revolting liar, a pusillanimous liar, a lying ass, a natural born liar, a liar by profession, a liar of living, a liar in the daytime, a liar in the nighttime, a dishonest, ignorant, corrupt and groveling crook.

—Kenneth McKellar

That over-educated Oxford s.o.b.

—Harry S Truman, of Senator William Fulbright

An empty cab drove up and Sarah Bernhardt got out.

—Arthur "Bugs" Baer

Sherard Blaw, the dramatist who had discovered himself, and who had given so ungrudgingly of his discovery to the world . . .

—Saki (H. H. Munro)

Westbrook Pegler built a reputation on invective:

[Quentin] Reynolds is a celebrity who has fallen in love with himself.

FALLACY

Fallacious reasoning was and still is the secret weapon of the professional persuader and is not used only by the inept logician. Knowledge of the devices, however, is useful not only for persuasion but also to help you identify and rebut a fallacy. The following are a few of the most common forms of logical fallacy. A good writer and speaker can use them to advantage if they are spiced with humor and uttered with tongue in cheek.

The *converse accident* is the term applied to a conclusion reached on the basis of an unrepresentative example. Aristotle called it a "sign" or "a single instance." Thus:

> I can see better with my one eye than with two eyes. You, with two eyes can only see one eye, but I, with one eye, can see your two eyes.
>
> —Victor Borge

> Peanuts fattening? Just look at the elephant.

> We have two ears and only one tongue in order that we may hear more and speak less.
>
> —Diogenes

> I can produce ten witnesses who did not see the defendant commit the crime.

The fallacy that because something is generally true, it is true in a special situation, was and still is known as *secundum quid*, from the Latin, "*A dicto simpliciter ad dictum secundum quid*," which translates literally as, "from the bare statement to a statement made for some reason."

> It's obvious that you will get on faster at the top than at the bottom, because there are more people at the bottom than at the top, so naturally the competition at the bottom is stiffer.
>
> —Ogden Nash

> I always hire older people. Statistics show that very few people die at ninety-nine or over.

> If absence makes the heart grow fonder, how some people must love their church.

CAUSE AND EFFECT

Metalepsis, from the Greek "substitution," was also known as *transumptio*, "assuming one thing from another," in Latin, and as *farfet* by Puttenham. Here you attribute a present situation to a remote cause, ignoring what has happened in between.

I curse the day that I was born that I might live to see my daughter marry an infidel.

I am glad that I am not a man, for then I should have to marry a woman.

—Mme. De Staël

In the United States there is more space where nobody is than where anybody is.
This is what makes America what it is.
—Gertrude Stein, *The Geographical History of America*

Wife: If you had really loved me, you would have married some other woman.

No wonder people don't come here—it's so crowded!
—Ray Van Cleaf

Coming to an irrelevant conclusion known as *ignoratio elenchi*, which is Latin for "ignorance of confutation," is one of several devices you'll find useful for avoiding an issue.

The best way to protect a wedding ring is to dip it in dishwater three times a day.
—Louise Grimes

My husband is a deceitful no-good. Last night he pretended to believe me when he knew I was lying.

ASSUMING THE CONCLUSION

Petitio principii, or begging the question, means coming to a conclusion from a premise that is not really proven itself. One variety of this fallacy is circular reasoning. Thus, poverty is good, since Americans have many freedoms, including the freedom to be unemployed and to starve.

THE RIGGED QUESTION

By posing a rigged question you require the person answering to admit something no matter how he answers. The most famous example is:

Have you stopped beating your wife?

An affirmative statement can also be rigged:

If the Republicans stop telling lies about us, we will stop telling the truth about them.

—Adlai Stevenson, 1952

Advertisers use this in a more subtle way:

Why take less?

Are you still following the Wall Street herd?

—Windsor Fund

What becomes a legend most?

—Blackglama

Sometimes with some evidential background:

Why were all of these leading package goods products advertised in *Newsweek* during 1976–1977?

AFTER THIS

Post hoc, ergo propter hoc ("after this, therefore because of this") is a common logical fallacy. Its essence is mistaking an event preceding another in time, for a cause. You can use this basic idea in a variety of situations:

> The time not to become a father is eighteen years before a world war.
>
> —E. B. White

> He was like a cock who thought the sun had risen to hear him crow.
>
> —George Eliot

Some superstitions are examples of this kind of fallacious reasoning: I walked under a ladder and soon after I broke my leg. Therefore my bad luck was caused by my walking under a ladder.

SIMPLISTICS

Simplistics is a device for avoiding a complicated situation by reducing it to the terms you desire. Thus, you'll discover that your oversimplification, the element of "it's self-evident," often provides a ring of truth:

> The Ten Commandments and the Sermon on the Mount contain my religion.
>
> —John Adams

> The whole art of government consists in the art of being honest.
>
> —Thomas Jefferson

> Late children, early orphans.
>
> —Benjamin Franklin, 1742

> If you wish to be a writer, write.
>
> —Epictetus

> So why shouldn't we allow the son of a millionaire to be a millionaire, if after all we allow the sons of workers to be workers?
>
> —Mellan Fernandes

I never think of the future. It comes soon enough.

—Albert Einstein

Only those who will risk going too far can possibly find out how far one can go.

—T. S. Eliot

Never learn to do anything. If you don't learn, you will always find someone else to do it for you.

—Mark Twain

And here logic melts the obvious:

Never argue at the dinner table, for the one who is not hungry always gets the best of the argument.

—Richard Whately

There has never been a statue erected in memory of someone who let well enough alone.

—Jules Ellinger

Work is the greatest thing in the world. So we should save some of it for tomorrow.

—Don Herold

I want you to remember that no bastard ever won a war by dying for his country. He won it by making the other poor dumb bastard die for his country.

—General George S. Patton

This day, too, will pass.

CHAPTER

FIGURES OF DICTION

WE HAVE NOTED THAT, HISTORICALLY, A VERY IMPORTANT facet of rhetoric as it was conceived by the Greeks and taught through the centuries was the "delivery." From Aristotle's time through the nineteenth century, rhetoric was principally for the orator, the clergyman, the lawyer, and the legislator. It was a prime tool, an almost exact science.

In one historic tradition, delivery (called *actio* by the Romans) was the fifth part of rhetoric—after invention, arrangement, style, and memory.

Everyone realized that the level and style of language and delivery should be appropriate to the message, the audience, and the speaker. The purpose is to create a milieu of communication—familiar or remote, down-to-earth or metaphysical, loud or soft-spoken.

In addition to the many devices available for the writer for effective communication, many more are available to the speaker. As an orator, you can use stress, pitch, melody, mimicry, or singsong to express nuances of meaning far more subtle, more emphatic, more emotive, more varied in a score of ways than just punctuation can convey on paper. The best known of the devices is stress. The Greeks and Romans also noted *aposiopesis* (becoming silent), *caesum* (cutting off), *correctio* (setting right), *aphaeresis* (omitting syllables), *prosthesis* (adding syllables), and *apostrophe* (addressing a personified thing or absent person). There are several ways you can phrase questions: you may make your question rhetorical or exclamatory, or use it to reproach; you may use a question to answer your own or someone else's question, to pretend, to start a discussion, or to state a fact.

Quotations open a way for you to provide authority or evidence, to bring the support of a renowned name or involve the voice of an imaginary person, an animal, an inanimate object, or the weight of history. The quotations you use may be in the form of a toast or an epitaph, in or out of context, doctored or paraphrased or humorously turned, or merely alluded to.

Exclamation is another powerful tool. Perhaps most dramatic of the variations in the voice, the exclamation may express enthusiasm, fear, horror, joy—any emotion you can contrive. A raised eyebrow, an inflection of the voice, can change your statement from an assertion to an equivocation or a denial. Sweet and pleasant modulation of your voice (the Greeks called it *tasis*, meaning "pitch") can play an important part in your delivery, where appropriate. In truth, rhetoric was designed in an unliterate age almost entirely for vocal communication.

So in many, if not most situations, a large number of the most powerful devices of expression are phonetic—although some of those described below are also applicable to writing. One advertiser makes this point:

> If you want to capture someone's attention, whisper.
> —Nuance perfume

and another notes:

> A new idea is delicate. It can be killed by a sneer or a yawn; it can be stabbed to death by a quip and worried to death by a frown on the right man's brow.
> —Charles Brower

STRESS AND STOPS

Stress is used to imply more than you have actually said. This use of emphasis was called *significatio* by the Romans (from the Latin "sign") and *reinforcer* by Puttenham.

A well-known illustration in the use of stress shows the variety of meanings which arise when you emphasize different words in the same sentence:

I never said he stole the money.
I NEVER said he stole the money.
I never SAID he stole the money.
I never said HE stole the money.
I never said he STOLE the money.
I never said he stole the MONEY.

A different type of emphasis is used in this advertisement for a New York department store:

***
That's how Altman's rates this be-furred B-eautiful wool coat.

THE ELOQUENCE OF SILENCE

Aposiopesis, translated as "becoming silent," is the device of the unfinished thought. Vittorio Emanuele Orlando, the Italian statesman who helped reshape the world in 1919, is quoted as saying:

Oratory is just like prostitution: You must have little tricks. One of my favorite tricks is to start a sentence and leave it unfinished. Everyone racks his brains and wonders what I was going to say.

It's just that . . . never mind.
—Edward Albee

The term applies as well to words not said, but which can

be inferred. Unfinished sentences are typical of spoken language, especially to avoid a threat:

If you don't wipe that smile off your face . . .

Sometimes making a correction of a statement during a speech can emphasize a point for you—giving the suggestion of greater thought or greater accuracy. The Greeks used a term *epanorthosis* meaning "setting straight"; the Romans called it *correctio*, meaning "setting right."

There be three things which are too wonderful for me, yea, four which I know not: the way of an eagle in the air; the way of a serpent upon a rock; the way of a ship in the midst of the sea; and the way of a man with a maid.

—Proverbs 30:18–19

The newspapers! Sir, they are the most villainous—licentious—abominable—infernal—Not that I ever read them—no—I make it a rule never to look into a newspaper.

—Richard Brinsley Sheridan

Ellipsis (from the Greek "leave out") shortens an expression by eliminating (or adding) a word or phrase. Here the verb is omitted:

And he to England shall along with you.

—William Shakespeare

Ellipsis is often used when you have to fit words to rhyme or rhythm: "What ship could live in such a sea? / What vessel bear the shock? / 'Ho! starboard part your helm-a-lee! / Ho! reef the maintop-gallant-tree with many a running block?' "

Parenthetical expressions are another form of detached construction that you can use to deemphasize, to make a point without seeming to make it.

So Justice Oberwaltzer—solemnly and didactically from his high seat to the jury . . .

—Theodore Dreiser

EXCLAMATION

The interjection as an exclamation, although more widely used in archaic writings, still holds a place in contemporary usage. Some grammarians view the interjection not as a part of speech in a sentence, but as a sentence in itself. Nor need you limit interjections to the ordinary ohs and ahs. "Wonderful!" "Terrible!" "Man oh man!" "Jiminy Cricket!" The emotional charge is what creates the exclamation.

The Greek term *apostrophe* is the device of stopping to address an absent person or thing or a stranger and is translated as "turning away." The Romans called it *aversio*, with the same translation; Puttenham labeled it *turne tale*. It is useful in calling attention to a statement, "like a rocket shooting into the air."

O tempora! O mores! [O what times! What morals!]

—Cicero

Oh, to have the gift to think for ourselves as we can think for others.

—A. O. Sabol

What an ocean is life! And how our barks get separated in beating through it!

—Thomas Jefferson

A more modern use of the exclamation is as a stopper. Walter Winchell used this effectively in his columns and radio programs. Here's a Joey Adams version:

Flash! Scientists have just proven that a man can be frozen in a state of suspended animation for four years without losing his job at the post office.

And as an advertisement:

Hark! the herald angels sing,
Beecham's Pills are just the thing;

> Peace on earth and mercy mild,
> Two for man and one for child.

Ecphonesis, from the Greek "to cry out," was called *exclamatio* by the Romans, and *outcrie* by Puttenham. It involves the sort of expression we normally punctuate with an exclamation point:

> Thou, too, sail on, O Ship of State!
> Sail on, O Union strong and great!
> Humanity with all its fears,
> With all the hopes of future years,
> Is hanging breathless on thy fate!
> —Henry Wadsworth Longfellow

> Gold! Gold! Gold! Gold!
> Bright and yellow, hard and cold.
> —Thomas Hood

How beautiful is victory, but how dear!
> —Louis Francis Boufflers

QUESTIONS IN MANY VARIETIES

Questions arouse attention by involving your audience. They can also perform the practical function of avoiding a positive statement when you don't want to assume full responsibility.

The most widely known of the question devices is the rhetorical question. The Greeks called it *erotesis*, translated simply as "a questioning"; the Romans called it *interrogatio*. This is a device that reshapes the meaning: Your question is no longer a question but a statement in the form of an interrogative sentence. The answer is already implied in the question. In this way you can create a double impact: as a question and as a statement—either positive or negative. And often it can be an exclamation.

Is not marriage an open question, when it is alleged, from the beginning of the world, that such as are in the institution wish to get out, and such as are out wish to get in?

—Ralph Waldo Emerson

The reverse rhetorical question is equally effective:

One does not ask of one who suffers: What is your country and what is your religion? One merely says: You suffer, this is enough for me; you belong to me and I shall help you.

Sometimes you can use the question to defend an attitude:

What is the Presidency worth to me if I have no country?

—Abraham Lincoln

What has posterity done for us?

—John Trumbull, 1782

Or to express an exclamation:

O Heavens! Is't possible a young maid's wits
Should be as mortal as an old man's life?

—*Hamlet,* IV, 159–160

Or a challenge, as this passage from the Bible:

Which of you by taking thought can add one cubit unto his stature?

—Matthew 6:27

And an advertiser uses it this way:

Test your business I.Q.
Q. The ranks of the unemployed are swelled with secretaries. True or false?

A question can be an answer to a question. When asked why he expended so much effort to discover the antipolio vaccine, Dr. Jonas Salk responded: "Why did Mozart compose music?"

Asking a question and then answering it yourself was a

device called *hypophora* (meaning "contrary motion") by the Greeks and *subjectio* (meaning "substitution") by the Romans.

Can one generation bind another and all others, in succession forever? I think not.

—Thomas Jefferson

What is matter? Never mind.
What is mind? No matter.

—*Punch*

Why fear death? Death is only a beautiful adventure.
—Charles Frohman, 1915. Last words of the American producer. He died in the torpedoing of the *Lusitania*.

Know thyself? If I knew myself, I'd run away.
—Johann Wolfgang von Goethe

The question can be used facetiously:

Why is the rocking chair a perfect symbol of the New Frontier? Because it provides a feeling of motion while not going anywhere.
—Republican comment about Kennedy administration

Why is a man more easily pacified than a woman? Because man was made out of soft earth, and woman out of a hard rib.
—Dosetai ben Jannai.

Love the sea? I dote upon it—from the beach.
—Douglas Jerrold

An advertiser uses the device in this way:

What Worries Consumers Most?

The high price of many products
The high cost of medical and hospital care
The poor quality of many products
The failure of many companies to live up to claims
made in their advertising

> The poor quality of after-sale service and repairs
> The feeling that many manufacturers don't care
>   about you
> > —Sentry Insurance

Or you can leave the answer unsaid:

> How long must it go on? How long must we suffer? Where is the end? What is the end?
> > —George William Norris

Asking a question in order to reproach (the Greeks called it *epiplexis* or *epitimesis*, for "rebuke," and the Romans *percontatio*, meaning "inquiry") is another way:

> Is there not blood enough upon your penal code that more must be poured forth to ascend to Heaven and testify against you?
> > —George Gordon Lord Byron

> I am a Jew. Hath not a Jew eyes? Hath not a Jew hands, organs, dimensions, senses, affections, passions; fed with the same food, hurt with the same weapons, subject to the same diseases, healed by the same means, warmed and cooled by the same winter and summer, as a Christian is?
> > —William Shakespeare, Shylock in
> > *The Merchant of Venice*

Or you can pose a challenge:

> Who says you can't speak another language in 60 days?
> > —Linguaphone for Languages

It is a technique that is now offered usually in a humorous vein to soften the impact of a reproach.

> The dessert was delicious. Did you buy it yourself?

> Don't you have a machine that puts food into the mouth and pushes it down?
> > —Nikita Khrushchev, to Vice-President Nixon,
> > noting inventions in the American model house
> > at the Moscow Fair, 1959

Are these the kind of skis that can be made into splints?

Why don't you speak for yourself, John?
> —Henry Wadsworth Longfellow,
> *The Courtship of Miles Standish*

Asking a question as a starting point for a comment is one of the simpler uses:

Is Wagner a human being at all? Is he not rather disease? He contaminates everything he touches—he has made music sick.
> —Friedrich Nietzsche

Does anyone seriously think that a real traitor will hesitate to sign a loyalty oath? Of course not. Really dangerous subversives will be caught by careful, constant, professional investigation, not by pieces of paper.
> —Adlai Stevenson

Here is how an advertiser uses it to attract a reader:

What in the world's gone wrong with the weather?
> —*National Geographic Magazine*

Sometimes as a writer or speaker you can answer a question or respond to a remark of a pretended interlocutor. The Latin term was *sermocinatio*, translated as "discussion," a variation of *prosopopoeia*.

I have been asked, "How do you grow old so easily?" I reply, "Very easily. I give all my time to it."
> —Rep. Emanuel Celler, on his eighty-third birthday

Ask not what the Kremlin wants. We know that. Soviet leaders want to run the world. And are working hard toward that end. Tell us instead what the U.S. wants and show us that the U.S. has the will, not just the power, to get it.
> —*U.S. News & World Report,* January 2, 1976

Advertisers use the device in this way:

Why a man's magazine now?
Because there isn't one. That's why.
> —*Esquire*

Shouldn't the motor of the best food processor last a lifetime?
Waring thinks so.

QUOTATIONS AND ALLUSIONS

Of course, there are many useful direct quotations. Less direct use of a quotation is an allusion—a reference to a well-known story or fact or even a myth. The basic requirement, of course, is that it be well-known to your audience, although not necessarily to everyone or even to *all* who are listening or reading. Usually you need not make reference to the source. You may refer to Watergate without having to explain what it signifies—some knowledge may be assumed.

Our aim is to recognize what Lincoln pointed out: The fact that there are some respects in which men are obviously not equal; but also to insist that there should be an equality of self-respect and of mutual respect, an equality of rights before the law, and at least an approximate equality in the conditions under which each man obtains the chance to show the stuff that is in him when compared to his fellows.

—Theodore Roosevelt

I believe with Franklin that freedom and free government depend upon an educated citizenry.

—Dwight D. Eisenhower

In a facetious vein, you can make joking allusions to well-known sayings:

People who live in chateaux
Shouldn't throw tomataux.

—John Madison Morton

In advertising:

Mumm's the word.

—Mumm's champagne

If at first you don't succeed, you may be out on your ear.

—D. L. Blair

What the Greeks called *prosopopoeia*, the Romans *conformatio* (Latin for "symmetrical forming") and Puttenham *counterfait in personation* is the device of speaking as someone else. Puttenham gives this example:

> . . . if we should fain King Edward the third, understanding how his successor Queen Mary had lost the town of Calais by negligence, should say: That which the sword won, the distaff lost.
>
> —quoted by George Puttenham

Here are some modern instances:

> Jack Kennedy's father: "Jack, what do you want as a career?"
> Jack Kennedy: "I want to be president."
> Jack Kennedy's father: "I know about that—but I mean when you grow up."
> —*Republican National Committee Magazine*

> The pessimist says, "It can't be done."
> The optimist says, "It can be done."
> The peptimist says, "I just did it."

Eidolopoeia was the Greek term for "formation of mental images." Here you pretend that a dead person is speaking. The ghost of Hamlet's father is the first example to come to mind:

> I am thy father's spirit,
> Doom'd for a certain term to walk the night,
> And for the day confin'd to fast in fires,
> Till the foul crimes done in my days of nature
> Are burnt and purg'd away.

Speaking as an animal or an inanimate object was called *fictio,* meaning "invention," by the Romans. The fables are largely couched in this way:

> A fly sat on the chariot wheel
> And said, "What a dust I raise."
> —Jean de La Fontaine

Thus Parkay's package saying, "the flavor is 'butter,' " is a recent use on television.

You might prefer to send a message in the form of a real or imaginary epitaph:

Die when I may, I want it said of me by those who knew me best, that I always plucked a thistle and planted a flower where I thought a flower would grow.

—Abraham Lincoln

I would have written of me on my stone: I had a lover's quarrel with the world.

—Robert Frost

Excuse my dust.

—Dorothy Parker

Asked to write an epitaph for a lady of many friendships, Robert Benchley offered these words:

"AT LAST SHE SLEEPS ALONE."

Some others:

The Body of Benjamin Franklin, Printer
(Like the cover of an old book,
Its contents torn out
And stript of its lettering and gilding),
Lies here, food for worms;
But the work shall not be lost,
For it will (as he believed) appear once more
In a new
And more elegant edition,
Revised and corrected
by the Author.

—Benjamin Franklin

Beneath this stone my wife doth lie:
Now she's at rest, and so am I.

—Boileau

> Misplacing—mistaking
> Misquoting—misdating
> Men, Manners, things and facts all.
> Here lies Sir Nathaniel Wralall

Or as a toast:

> To the Bachelor—who is always free!
> To the Husband—who sometimes may be!

Paroemia, the Greek word for "byword," and *paradiegesis,* the Greek term for "incidental narrative," involve using a proverb, quotation, or anecdote as the basis for a comment.

> As the Spanish proverb says, He who would bring home the wealth of the Indies must carry the wealth of the Indies with him. So it is in travelling: a man must carry knowledge with him, if he would bring home knowledge.
> —Samuel Johnson, quoted in Boswell's *Life of Johnson*

> There is a French saying "Love is the dawn of marriage, and marriage is the sunset of love."

Like a question, a quotation may be followed by a comment:

> I find that the remark, " 'Tis distance lends enchantment to the view" is no less true of the political than of the natural world.
> —Franklin Pierce

> One verse of Micah . . . I am very fond of . . . "to do justly and to love mercy and to walk humbly with thy God." That to me is the essence of religion.
> —Theodore Roosevelt

You may also employ a quotation to support a statement:

> This is not a time to keep the facts from the people—to keep them complacent. To sound the alarm is not to panic but to seek action from an aroused public. For, as Dante once said:

The hottest places in hell are reserved for those who, in a time
of great moral crisis, maintain their neutrality.
                                                            —John F. Kennedy

In the words of Woodrow Wilson: "We must neither run with
the crowd nor deride it—but seek sober counsel for it—and for
ourselves."
                                                            —John F. Kennedy

To a man who was commenting on the good fortune of Andrew
Carnegie, Samuel Clemens had a quick response. "But after
all," said the man in a superior tone, "like all these great fortunes, Carnegie's money is tainted."
"Yes," agreed Clemens, " 'taint yours, and 'taint mine."

We may say of angling as Dr. Boteler said of strawberries:
Doubtless God could have made a better berry, but doubtless
God never did, and so (if I might be judge) God never did make
a more calm, quiet, innocent recreation than angling.
                                                            —Izaak Walton

On the whole, quotation adds a new dimension to your
writing: a sort of wider vocabulary. Dictionaries of quotations
abound with ideas so well put in content and form that the
ordinary writer must work hard indeed to compete with them.
Often repeating a statement in a different context gives it a
status or meaning not originally presented.

One of Congress's more pompous members remarked to Horace
Greeley, "I am a self-made man." To which Greeley replied,
"Well sir, that relieves the Almighty of a great responsibility."

You may use a quotation out of context to provide a diver-
sion or a laugh or a retort.

A funny thing happened to me on the way to the White
House . . .
                                                            —Adlai Stevenson

A funny thing happened to me on my way to Cuba.
                                    —Adlai Stevenson, introducing John F. Kennedy

The ancient sage who concocted the maxim, "Know thyself," might have adopted, "Don't tell anyone."

—H. L. Mencken

If Patrick Henry thought taxation without representation was so terrible, he should see it with representation.

—*United Mine Workers Journal*

Adapting or paraphrasing a proverb or quotation is one of the most common of all devices; Adlai Stevenson used it frequently.

I have finally figured out what the Republican orators mean by what they call "moderate progressivism." All they mean is: "Don't just do something; stand there."

We cannot afford to be penny-wise and people-foolish.

And from George Bernard Shaw:

An army and navy in hand is worth ten Leagues of Nations in the bush.

Similarly:

What is good for algae is not necessarily good for Lake Erie.

He puts off until tomorrow everything he has already put off until today.

Blessed are those who can give without remembering and take without forgetting.

—Walter C. Parker

An advertiser uses it this way:

If you appreciate golden eggs, you don't kill the goose. You find a gander.

—Pullman, Inc.

Misquotation—poking fun at a proverb, quotation, or

cliché by changing a few words, a sort of quotational pun—invites more smiles.

Keep your eye on the ball, your shoulder to the wheel, and your ear to the ground . . . now try to work in that position.

We have met the enemy and he is us.

—Pogo (by Walt Kelly)

Everybody talks about the weather but the only people who do anything about it are hotelkeepers. They pray.

—Gertrude Berg

Sometimes a small loan is just enough to tide you under.

—*Changing Times*

He who laughs lasts.

Blessed are the young, for they shall inherit the national debt.

—Herbert Hoover

He's the kind of friend you can depend on—always around when he needs you.

—General Features Corp.

Eat, drink, and be merry, for tomorrow ye diet.

—William Gilmore Beymer

Suggesting a proverb can also make an audience remember your idea:

In the all important world of family relations, three words are almost as powerful as the famous "I love you." They are, "maybe you're right."

—Oren Arnold

And there is also denial of a quotation:

People should execrate me for things I have said, not for the things that fools say I have said.

—George Bernard Shaw

GRAMMATICAL AND OTHER IRREVERENCES

MOST WRITING FOLLOWS A BASIC SET OF RULES THAT ARE recited in English Composition I. The predicate follows the subject, and so forth, with some variations. But by taking advantage of several devices noted by rhetoricians you can change the ordinary patterns radically.

INVERSION

A number of these structural aberrations are grammatical inversions—that is, you arrange your words in a strikingly unusual way. This is an attention-getting device termed by the Greeks *anastrophe,* or "turning back." The Romans called it *reversio* or *perversio,* meaning "inversion." It is one of several devices classified as *hysteron proteron,* which in Greek means "the latter put as the former." Inversion emphasizes the element at the beginning of the sentence and serves to draw attention to the whole expression. One tongue-in-cheek example is Winston Churchill's response to "Never end a sentence with a preposition."

This is the kind of impertinence up with which I will not put.

Some common forms of inversion:

1. You place the object at the beginning of the sentence:

Talent Mr. Micawber has; capital Mr. Micawber has not.

—Charles Dickens

2. You place the predicate adjective at the beginning of the sentence:

Rude am I in my speech . . .

—Shakespeare, *Othello*

3. You place the adverb or adverbial phrase at the beginning of the sentence:

Eagerly I wished the morrow.

—Edgar Allan Poe

4. You place both the preposition and the predicate at the beginning of the sentence:

In went Mr. Pickwick.

—Charles Dickens

5. You follow the noun with the adjective:

Once upon a midnight dreary . . .

—Edgar Allan Poe

With fingers weary and worn . . .

—Thomas Hood

6. You employ detached constructions in which parts of a sentence seem to be broken off from the main part:

June stood in front, fighting off this idle curiosity—a little bit of a thing, as somebody said, "All hour and spirit."

—John Galsworthy

She was lovely. All of her—delightful.

—Theodore Dreiser

ZEUGMA I

A handy device is use of a single word, usually a verb, to govern several words so that it applies to each in a different sense. This is *zeugma* in Greek (translated as "yoking"). Puttenham called it *single supply*. You'll find zeugma useful for creating a pun, as we shall see. Henry Peacham cites as an example of zeugma:

Pride oppresseth humility; hatred love; cruelty compassion.

An advertiser makes this point:

Finally solar energy is generating heat instead of confusion.
—City Investing Co.

In another form, you can have one subject serve many verbs. This variation is called *diazeugma*, meaning "disjoining":

. . . he bites his lip and starts,
Stops on a sudden, looks upon the ground,
Then lays his finger on his temple; straight
Springs out into fast gait; then stops again . . .
—Shakespeare, *Henry VIII*

An alternative is one verb incongruent with one or more subjects. This was called *syllepsis*, meaning "taking together." Puttenham calls this *double supply*:

Nothing is often a good thing to do, and always a clever thing to say.
—Will Durant

I had rather be right than President.
—Henry Clay

You can also repeat similar clauses, each with a different subject and verb. This was termed *hyperzeugma* by the Greeks, the opposite of zeugma, in which one verb serves several objects. This example of *anaphora* (a type of hyperzeugma in which the same word is repeated at the beginning of successive clauses) is sometimes cited:

We shall not flag or fail. We shall fight in France, we shall fight on the seas and oceans, we shall fight with growing confidence and growing strength in the air, we shall defend our island, whatever the cost may be, we shall fight on the landing grounds, we shall fight in the fields and in the streets, we shall fight in the hills; we shall never surrender.

—Winston Churchill

Or in a more commonplace setting:

A good woman inspires a man,
A brilliant woman interests him,
A beautiful woman fascinates him—
The sympathetic woman gets him.

—Helen Rowland

VOICE CHANGES

A sudden change from passive to active voice or the reverse is another method by which you can gain attention:

The register of his burial was signed by the clergyman, the clerk, the undertaker, and the chief mourner. Scrooge signed it.

—Charles Dickens

By using such a change you achieve a certain element of surprise. In this way you are placing the emphasis on the second sentence.

ABOUT CONJUNCTIONS

Omitting the conjunction gives you a staccato effect. The Greeks termed this *asyndeton* (meaning "unconnected"). The Romans called it *dissolutio,* and Puttenham, *loose language.*

Sighted sub; sank same.

—Lt. Donald F. Hasa, 1942

Enemy advances, we retreat; enemy halts, we harass; enemy tires, we attack; enemy retreats, we pursue.

—Mao Tse-tung, strategy for war, quoted by
Dwight D. Eisenhower, 1963

Laws too gentle are seldom obeyed; too severe, seldom executed.
—Benjamin Franklin

On the other hand, extensive use of the conjunction—called *polysyndeton,* the opposite of asyndeton—is also sometimes effective:

The heaviest rain, and snow, and hail, and sleet, could boast of the advantage over him in only one respect.
—Charles Dickens

Neither snow, nor rain, nor heat, nor gloom of night stays these couriers from the swift completion of their appointed rounds.
—Inscription on Manhattan
Post Office, adapted from the
Histories of Herodotus

ZEUGMA II

As we have noted, zeugma often involves a simple pun. Thus, in Pope's "Rape of the Lock" the different meanings of the verb are put to work:

. . . whether the nymph
Shall stain her Honour or her new Brocade
Or lose her heart or necklace at a Ball

Charles Dickens uses the device:

And May's mother always stood on her gentility; and Dot's mother never stood on anything but her aching littling feet.

PUNS

The irreverent playing with words as a source of wit, humor, and criticism is the subject of diatribes from the earliest times, yet it persists in the most facile gags, the easiest retorts, the most serious comments. The Greeks had a word for it, of course: *paronomasia,* meaning playing on the sounds and meaning of words.

One of the most popular kinds of punning is the homonymic pun, which depends on two words sounding alike but having different meanings:

Censorship: An idea fostered by people who want to stick their no's into everyone's business.

—Joan I. Welsh

The pun has been regarded as the "lowest form of humor" through the centuries. Nonetheless it is widely used. Ben Jonson was a master at it, and of Jonson's punning John Dryden said that it was the "lowest and most gravel kind . . . which we call clenches, of which *Every Man in His Humour* is infinitely full." Dryden also criticized Shakespeare for this fault. The pun had some defenders, though. According to Dr. Johnson, "The pun is one of the smaller excellencies of lively conversation." Dr. Johnson then offered to make a pun on any subject. Someone suggested "the king." His response: "The King is not a subject."

Shakespeare uses thousands. This is just one:

Golden lads and girls all must,
As chimney-sweepers, come to dust.

—*Cymbeline*

And in *Othello*:

Put out the light and then put out the light—
that is, snuff the candle and then smother Desdemona.

A blunt eighteenth-century commentary deploring the vices of the times concludes:

All Houses are now Ale-houses; some men's Paradise is a Pair o' Dice; the holy State of Matrimony is Matter o' Money. Was it thus in the Days of Noah? Ah No!

—*Spectator,* No. 409

Peace is much more precious than a piece of land.

—Anwar Sadat

Modern punning makes the most of American idiom:

Do your homemade cookies look as if they came from a broken home?

—Joan Rivers

You could get rich manufacturing crutches for lame excuses.

—Mary H. Waldrip, *Dawson County, Ga., Advertiser and News*

It appears that we're sending arms to just about everybody but Venus de Milo.

—Fletcher Knebel, *Reader's Digest*

He who slings mud generally loses ground.

—Adlai Stevenson

The one thing children wear out faster than shoes is parents.

—Quoted in *The Saturday Evening Post*

Golf: a game in which the balls lie on the ground and the players lie in the clubhouse.

Court—where a suit is pressed and a man can be taken to the cleaners.

A Democratic convention is always a political party.

Advertising copywriters show no reluctance in using it:

The chemistry's just right at Chemical.

—Chemical Bank

Altman's Valen-timed sales for men.

Waterford Crystal advertises its saltcellars:

When it pours, it reigns.

Quail—a gift in good taste.

The best gifts grow on trees.

> —Advertisement for fruit

Get a horse at OTB.

Are you a yes-man or a know-man?

> —*Wall Street Journal* advertisement

A billion dollars in assets doesn't make us great—it makes us grateful.

> —The Greenpoint Savings Bank

IBM cards: working paper . . . not paper work.

> —International Business Machines Corp.

Cheese bored?

> —*International Gourmet*

At a motel: "We welcome members of the pet set."

> —Charlotte Stern

In a travel agency: "Have you a yen to go to Japan?"

> —Camille Edwards

Next to myself, I like BVD best.

> —BVD (Bradley, Voorhees and Day)

Here are some more examples to give you an idea of how to construct plays on words:

They pick a President and then for four years they pick on him.

> —Adlai Stevenson

Would you say a man who has had a hair transplant has a "re-seeded hairline?"

> —Jacklyn Nation

Muttonchop sideburns are appearing on all ages—from young kids to old goats.

> —Quoted in *Drovers Journal*

It's one of those camps that are run strictly by the book—your checkbook.

A stage is what many a teen-age girl thinks she should be on, when actually it's something she's going through.

—Earl Mathes

She is descended from a long line that her mother listened to.

—Gypsy Rose Lee

Gross exaggeration is 144 times as exaggerated as ordinary exaggeration.

And even in politics, there was Barry Goldwater's slogan in 1964.

In your heart you know he's right.

Many puns are based on the understanding of one word in two different senses:

I wasted time and now doth time waste me.

—*Richard II*

An archaeologist is the best husband any woman can have: the older she gets, the more interested he is in her.

—Agatha Christie

Watching my figure is rough on me; the more I watch it, the more I see!

—Ruth Chadwick

He who believes that where there's smoke there's fire hasn't tried cooking on a camping trip.

—*Changing Times*

I once worked as a salesman and was very independent. I took orders from no one.

—Gerald Barzan

Killing time is murder on the installment plan.

The first thing that strikes a visitor in Paris is a taxi.

A family tree is the only tree nobody wants to be shady.

SLIPS OF THE TONGUE

Three types of slips of the tongue lend themselves to deliberate—or nondeliberate—effect on communication: the Freudian slip, the malapropism, and the spoonerism.

THE FREUDIAN SLIP

The Freudian slip, a slip of the tongue that reveals or appears to reveal the subconscious, received attention when President Gerald Ford was introduced at a 1976 election rally as Mr. Fraud. But you may utilize the Freudian slip intentionally, with or without a correction.

Some people drive as though determined that no accident will be prevented if they can help it.

The slip is more evident in sentence structure:

Before I start my speech I'd like to say something.

Ladies and gentlemen, I am not going to bore you with a speech today, but I will present to you a man who will.
—Chairman, introducing a speaker

I hope you can come, Senator, because all of us would like to hear the dope from Washington.
—Quoted by Kenneth B. Keating

You'll never know what your sermon meant to me. Why, it was just like water to a drowning man.

MALAPROPISMS

Misusing a word in an attempt to appear learned receives its name from Mrs. Malaprop, a character in Richard Brinsley Sheridan's popular play *The Rivals*, written in 1775. Mrs. Malaprop's enthusiasm for misuse of similar-sounding words earned her the name, which derives from the French *mal à propos*—inappropriate. The Greeks called it *acyron*, meaning "incorrect phraseology"; the Romans called it *improprietas*; Puttenham called it *uncouthe*. Mrs. Malaprop says, for example: "Now don't attempt to extirpate yourself from the matter: you know I have proof controvertible of it."

The malapropism is not strictly a rhetorical device, but it *is* a means through which you can add humor to a thought and through which you may have your thought noticed and repeated. You might find it handy, for instance, in defining a character. Shakespeare used the device in *Much Ado About Nothing*:

A villain! Thou wilt be condemned into everlasting redemption for this.

Sometimes, obviously, a malapropism is inadvertent. Pierre Salinger is quoted as describing John F. Kennedy as a "vociferous reader."

Purposeful use of the malapropism can be an effective device to inspire quotation:

He is suffering from bottle fatigue.

He is one of those political candidates who refuses to answer any question on the grounds that it will eliminate him.

It is said that Socrates died from an overdose of wedlock.

In some states they no longer hang murderers. They kill them by elocution.

—Will Rogers

It was a case of mistaken nonentity.

His remarks are not German to the discussion.

My wife tells me I'm an invertebrate smoker.

—*Indianapolis City Magazine*

Anheuser Busch advertisements use the device:

I can say that without fear of extradition.

A collection of malapropisms was assembled by Norton Mockridge in his *Fractured English*:

The English language is going through a resolution.

I was so surprised you could have knocked me over with a fender.

He treats me like dirt on his feet.

My father is retarded on a pension.

I rode an alligator to the top of the Empire State Building.

Sometimes a pun is intended:

Governor Shapp of Pennsylvania, presented with a pot of still whiskey made by the Michter's distillery in Schaefferstown, Pa., said, "Two pints of this will make one cavort."

—Earl Wilson

To err is Truman.

She's not her old sylph.

The filibusterers in Congress are organizing a Federal Tirade Commission.

She has a nice sense of rumor.

—John H. Cutler

Among contributions to *Verbatim*, a magazine about

words, we find a restaurant menu that offers lamb chops "cooked to your likeness." And one more comic lapse:

He was arrested for driving in an erotic manner.

—W. W. Viertel

CARRY-OVERS

Carry-over sounds or the slurring of sounds can be a device interesting enough to catch the attention of readers or listeners. A sign on newly planted grass read:

Help keep lawn order!

And the addition of one letter produced this amusing example:

Why don't they put ash trays where the ash strays?

And in an advertisement:

For cuts, scrapes and all skinjuries.

—Unguentine

Dropping in on an auction sale to see what was going-gone.

—Edward Arten, *Reader's Digest*

The actress reached success by attireless effort.

A variation is the "carry-away," where you construct a play on words through the addition or subtraction of letters:

Anger is one letter short of danger.

Only one letter separates fiend from friend.

Southern Comfort makes the most of a missing letter and a miss:

Sip into something comfortable.

Every Little Crook and Nanny

—Film title

STRAYING LETTERS

The spoonerism, named for Reverend William A. Spooner, is an apparently inadvertent misplacing of letters or syllables in two or more words:

He dealt a blushing crow.

Dr. Spooner was warden of New College, Oxford, in 1879, when he announced the hymn: "Kinquering congs their titles take." His expression "half-warmed fish" for "half-formed wish" gave his name to this form of mispronunciation. Some that are widely quoted:

Your tutor tells me you have hissed all the mystery lectures and tasted nearly three worms.

—W. H. Auden

A drama critic is a man who leaves no turn unstoned.

—George Bernard Shaw

The term for substituting one sound or letter for another within a word is *antisthecon*. You can find practical uses for adaptations of this device. Notice how some advertising copywriters use the misplaced letter:

Rhapsody in brew.

—Beer ad

A pitcher of contentment.

—Lipton's Iced Tea

Better laid than ever.

—Sign at a poultry farm

CHAPTER

LANGUAGE AS A DEVICE

THE DEVICES OF TRADITIONAL RHETORIC DEAL WITH IMAGERY, sound, structure, or diction. But, in addition, you'll find it handy to know about some useful devices of stylistics and communication that involve the choice of language and vocabulary. Of these, many have long been recognized, but a few are modern innovations.

There is a generation gap in language, as in other elements of our society. The post-World War I children are often shocked by the common language of the post-World War II children. Their grandparents would have been shocked by mention of a mattress. Louis Kronenberger noted: "One generation's pleasure is the next generation's embarrassment." Geography, educational level, ethnic background, as well as the age of your audience are thus important considerations in conveying an effective message.

Some writers—particularly those in academia—resort to what one critic calls Cadillac prose. Usually this style sounds pompous, but if your words are used correctly, you can demonstrate your erudition, in spite of the relative opacity of the prose.

There have been put before us a host of proposals for improving the performance of our schools. The proposals run the full gamut, from the plain postulation that the surest way of attaining quality education in the schools as they now stand is through large infusions of new funds, to advocacy of such gimmicks as vouchers and "deschooling," which would, in effect, put an end to the public schools as we have known them. Somewhere in between these extremes is the movement for "alternative schools."

—Albert Shanker

Sometimes resorting to a single, little-known word can give you the same effect. While he was in public life, Spiro Agnew made much of unusual words as a means of attracting attention to his speeches—many of them against liberal intellectuals. He refers to enemies as "troglodytes" (primitive cave dwellers). This is a typical approach:

A spirit of national masochism prevails, encouraged by an effete corps of impudent snobs who characterize themselves as intellectuals.

Sometimes he employed alliteration:

. . . nattering nabobs of negativism.

We could find no author for this old parody of "Twinkle, Twinkle, Little Star" in pompous language:

The Little Star

Scintillate scintillate, globule orific,
Fain would I fathom thy nature's specific.
Loftily poised in ether capacious,
Strongly resembling a gem carbonaceous.

When torrid Phœbus refuses his presence
And ceases to lamp with fierce incandescence,
Then you illumine the regions supernal,
Scintillate, scintillate, semper nocturnal.

Then the victim of hospiceless peregrination
Gratefully hails your minute coruscation.
He could not determine his journey's direction
But for your bright scintillating protection.

The New York Times uses the device to call attention to its new books. This is the headline:

For the Literate, the Cacographer,[1] the Orthoepist,[2] Logophile[3] and the Bewildered.

(1) One who spells badly; (2) One skilled in pronunciation; (3) One who loves words.

Almost automatically we must, and usually do, adjust the level of a conversation to our estimation of the audience: adult or child, professional or merchant, professor or student, the boys' or the women's club. But we must also consider the larger audience. When presidential candidate Jimmy Carter was interviewed by *Playboy*, his language included such words as "screw" and "shack-up"—not acceptable to a large part of the general American public.

To be effective—and remembered—a communication must first be received and digested. But the writer or speaker's ego —the desire to sound important—and habit are the source of much lack of communication in business and in everyday affairs.

EUPHEMISM

The art of saying something delicate or unpleasant in words that are agreeable, or at least not offensive, involves a whole technology of rhetoric. Among other things, it requires tact, politeness, indirection. One commentator illustrates it this way:

The evolution over the years of a civilized mental health service has been marked by periodic changes in terminology. The madhouse became the lunatic asylum; the asylum made way for the mental hospital—even if the building remained the same. Idiots, imbeciles and the feeble-minded became low, medium and high-grade mental defectives. All are now to be lumped together as patients of severely subnormal personality. The insane became persons of unsound mind, and are now to be mentally-ill patients. As each phrase develops the stigmata of popular prejudice, it is abandoned in favor of another, sometimes less precise than the old. Unimportant in themselves, these changes of name are the signposts of progress.

—New Statesman and Nation

There is of course a Greek term for this, *euphemismus*, meaning "to speak fair." Puttenham calls it *curry favell*, a corruption of an archaic word for flatterer, or, alternatively, *soother*. Euphemism is necessary for some audiences and a matter of tact in some situations.

You'll probably find euphemisms most necessary in four areas: morals, religion, illness, and government. Some publications will not mention death; they say instead that someone passed away. Most avoid four-letter words, and many refer to rape as an "assault." A bastard was a "love child" until fairly recently.

In the House of Commons, some epithets are specifically forbidden: "liar," "traitor," "coward," "jackass," "dog," "swine," "rat." Substitutes have been created.

Often you can use euphemisms ironically:

For all her declination toward the horizontal, Sally Jay is not all bed. In her ruefully recounted odyssey among the oddballs, she is often comically appealing.

—Time magazine, movie review

CONNOTATION

Powerful expression is often created by using words that have an emotional appeal that goes far beyond their definitions:

We need not take shelter when someone cries "Radical!"
—William E. Borah

"Segregation" is such an active word that it suggests someone is trying to segregate somebody else. So the word "apartheid" was introduced. Now it has such a stench in the nostrils of the world, they are referring to "autogenous development."

—Alan Paton

The term . . . "socialized medicine" was constantly used by [my] opposition in an attempt to confuse the provisions of the national health insurance program.

—Harry S Truman

Often you might decide that it is the unpleasant word that best conveys the meaning:

The trusts and combinations—the communism of self.

—Grover Cleveland

Segregation is adultery of an illicit intercourse between injustice and immorality.

—Martin Luther King

The epithet beautiful is used by surgeons to describe operations which their patients describe as ghastly, by physicists to describe methods of measurement which leave sentimentalists cold, by lawyers to describe cases which ruin all the parties to them, and by lovers to describe the objects of their infatuation, however unattractive they may appear to the unaffected spectator.

—George Bernard Shaw

It seems to me sad that "politics" and "politician" are so often epithets and words of disrespect and contempt, and not without justification, in the land of Jefferson and in a government by the governed.

—Adlai Stevenson

I just want to lobby for God.

—Billy Graham

The greatest meliorator of the world is selfish, huckstering trade.
—Ralph Waldo Emerson, *Society and Solitude,* 1870

Frequently you can rouse strong emotion by associating ordinary words in a way calculated to shock:

Fox hunting is the pursuit of the uneatable by the unspeakable.

. . . these Buddhist barbecues.
—Madame Ngo Dinh Nhu, referring to Buddhist monks who burned themselves to death in public protest

There are no "white" or "colored" signs on the foxholes or graveyards of battle.
—John F. Kennedy

That log house did me more good in politics than anything I ever said in a speech.
—John Nance Garner

There is no such thing as "soft sell" and "hard sell." There is only "smart sell" and "stupid sell."
—Charles Brower

THE VOCABULARY OF INSPIRATION

Inspiration, patriotism, and chauvinism share a special vocabulary. There is the inscription on the Liberty Bell:

Proclaim liberty throughout all the land unto all the inhabitants thereof.
—Leviticus, 25:10

Courage is a good word. It has a ring. It is a substance that other people, who have none, urge you to have when all is lost. To have courage, one must first be afraid. The deeper the fear, the more difficult the climb toward courage.
—Jim Bishop

If I were to select a watchword that I would have every young man write above his door and on his heart, it would be that good word "fidelity."
—Benjamin Harrison

We shared an audacious dream—and launched a brave enterprise.

—Adlai Stevenson

Sometimes it requires a whole sentence to create an emotional picture:

Like an armed warrior, like a plumed knight, James G. Blaine marched down the halls of American Congress and threw his shining lance full and fair against the brazen foreheads of the defamers of his country, and the maligners of his honor.

—Robert G. Ingersoll, in nominating James
Blaine for President, 1876

Don't join the book burners. Don't think you are going to conceal thoughts by concealing evidence that they ever existed.

—Dwight D. Eisenhower

AESOPIAN LANGUAGE

Both domestic and international politics have created a special set of meanings for the special needs of propaganda. Here the technique of the writer or speaker is to redefine words, phrases, and slogans to convey new meanings that are different from those we have long understood. These distortions drown thinking in responses stimulated by words that already have an accepted emotional pattern. We accept new terminologies as rapidly as press agentry can create them.

Government borrowing and spending, associated with "debt," is now "deficit spending," associated with business stimulation. The simple word "welfare," as used in the Consitution, which once meant the good of the nation, now refers to a program to mitigate poverty. A comment on the language of liberals is made by an ex-president:

Out of these slogans and phrases and new meanings of words come vague promises and misty mirages, such as "security from the cradle to the grave." In action they will frustrate those basic human impulses to production which alone make a dynamic nation.

—Herbert Hoover

Aesopian language is defined as dissembling language, in which words that seem to convey an innocent meaning really mean something else. Certain expressions become code words. Aesopian language is a necessity in government, where virtually everything must be viewed in terms of "public relations." Since Woodrow Wilson, at least, there has been a "reliable source" at the White House. In the Nixon and Ford eras the source of information at the State Department was the "senior American official." That famed institution, "a senior American officer," flourished during the tenure of Secretary of State Henry Kissinger. The mythical official actually was a device. Without explanation or further clues to his identity, the "senior American officer traveling on Kissinger's plane" became the attributed source of thousands of stories charting the progress Mr. Kissinger was making in his negotiations.

Thus, a Kissinger view of things was made known to the world while the Secretary himself diplomatically managed to avoid being quoted directly. The disappearance of "senior," as some called him, was made known to reporters aboard the official plane one day when they were informed that henceforth they should quote only "state department officials."

The same words may have a different effect or special meanings on different audiences. Thus, in the pre-World War II era, and later in the Middle East, in the Congo, and in other trying times and places, there was a common comment:

It depends whom you're neutral for.

William Safire explained in *The New York Times* the use of words with special connotations:

For example, the code words for a Palestinian state on Israel's border have long been "legitimate rights," just as the code words for not returning lands won in 1967 are "defensible borders." These are not diplomatic niceties; to many the phrases carry the same force as "final solution."

When President Anwar Sadat issued an invitation to a meeting in Cairo, *The New York Times* reported that he saw this as an opportunity "for the Arabs to secure a 'peace based on justice'—a code phrase for acceptable concessions from Israel."

The annual Doublespeak Award made by the National Council of Teachers of English has noted these examples:

radiation enhancement weapon [for neutron bomb]
—Department of Energy, The Pentagon

Society for the Investigation of Human Ecology [for conducting experiments in deprivation and human behavior control]
—Central Intelligence Agency

An unfortunate choice of design measures together with less than conventional precautions [as the cause of the Teton Dam disaster which caused fourteen deaths]
—Investigating panel

district work period [for its recess]
—House of Representatives

The vocabulary of the Vietnam War included "police action" for the destruction of villages, "technical assistance" for actual fighting in the boondocks, "incursions" for attacks in Cambodia. Flights over North Vietnam were "protective reaction strikes."

At home the "ghetto" is the "inner city," the poor are "the disadvantaged." The "undeveloped nations" became the "underdeveloped nations." During the Watergate investigation lies became "inoperative statements"; misdemeanors were "extralegal," misdeeds were "wrong in that time frame" or "at that point in time."

Imperialism is thus defined:

> The mission of the United States is one of benevolent assimilation.
>
> —William McKinley, 1898

A typical report of an unsuccessful negotiation is:

> Richard bleakly described the conversation as a "frank and vigorous exchange of views"—diplomatese for failure.

On the world scene, the Soviet Union made semantics a conscious tool of their expansion policy, especially during the 1960s. In many areas, the Soviet rationale is impossible to defend in terms of plain facts. To overcome this forensic problem, the communists devised a simple technique: They made the "good" words mean what they wanted them to mean. Thus peace, freedom, democracy—all words suggestive of progressive, reasonable government—were adapted to the Soviet purpose. Language is a weapon; Stalin defined it as "an instrument of struggle." Says one British writer, Edward Cranshaw:

> The language of communism . . . is not so much a means of explaining to an unbeliever what communism means, but an armory of weapons and tools intended to produce support or dissolve opposition to communist policies on the part of people either hostile or indifferent to them. The meaning of a communist word is not what you think it says, but what effect it is intended to produce.

Thus, too, if the world wants peace, the communists offer "peaceful coexistence," loosely defined or not defined at all. For a world that wants freedom, the Soviet Union has it, in its own variation. Freedom in "capitalist countries" is the freedom to starve. Status quo involves change. Peace is the acceptance of Soviet will. Work under "capitalism" is exploitation, under "socialism" freedom. A protective Western force requested by a threatened nation is an invading army, while a

Soviet invasion is "liberation." Inspection of disarmament becomes spying, and so on.

THE LANGUAGE OF BUREAUCRACY

Gobbledygook is the language of bureaucrats—disdained, denounced, denigrated—and generally should be avoided by the careful writer or speaker. Its chief uses, it would seem, are obfuscation and avoidance of the need to interpret regulations and legalese. Basically, it is a means of avoiding responsibility for interpreting a law, a regulation, or an order. A great authority on the use of English language, Winston Churchill comments:

> Let us have an end of such phrases as these: "It is also of importance to bear in mind the following considerations . . ." or "consideration should be given to the possibility of carrying into effect . . ." Most of these woolly phrases are mere padding, which can be left out.
>
> —Winston Churchill

Here are some examples:

AMF, Inc. is receiving a $3.9 million modification to a previously awarded negotiated firm fixed-price letter contract to purchase additional MK-82 Mod. 1 bomb bodies.

[Translated in its time as: "More bombs for Vietnam."]

One anecdote recalled by *Verbatim* is illustrative:

Q: Describe the injury as you saw it.
A: He had an extravasation of serous fluid into the soft tissues of the optic region causing extensive discoloration.
Q: Do you mean he had a black eye?
A: Yes.

A retort of sorts is offered by a service station attendant who took care of the doctor's flat tire: "The difficulty is a collapsed aerostatic perimeter," he reported.

Here's a paragraph from a book by a noted sociologist quoted in the *Princeton Alumni Weekly*:

Motoric reproduction processes. The third major component of modeling phenomena involves the utilization of symbolic representations of modeled patterns in the form of imaginal and verbal contents to guide overt performances. It is assumed that reinstatement of representational schemes provides a basis for self-instruction on how component responses must be combined and sequenced to produce new patterns of behavior. The process of representational guidance is essentially the same as response learning under conditions where a person behaviorally follows an externally depicted pattern or is directed through a series of instructions to enact novel response sequences. The only difference is that, in the latter cases, performance is directed by external cues whereas, in delayed modeling behavioral reproduction, it is monitored by symbolic counterparts of absent stimuli.

Within a few months of taking office, President Jimmy Carter was struggling with the problem. His response was an order that federal regulations be written "in plain English for a change." Cited as a horrible example of bureaucratese:

We respectfully petition, request, and entreat that due and adequate provision be made, this day and the date hereinafter subscribed, for the satisfying of these petitioners' nutritional requirements and for the organizing of such methods of allocation and distribution as may be deemed necessary and proper to assure the reception by and for said petitioners of such quantities of baked cereal products as shall, in the judgment of the aforesaid petitioners, constitute a sufficient supply thereof.

[Translation: "Give us this day our daily bread."]

Government writing workshops immediately instituted courses in writing intelligibly. The chief problem discovered was that the writers did not understand what they were writing and thus could not translate such gobbledygook as:

. . . consumer credit other than open end which is extended on an account by use of credit card shall be subject to the requirements of 226.7(a),(6),(7),(8), and (9); 226.7(b)(1)(I), (II),(III) . . .

Recent laws, which require that "plain English" be used in legal documents such as bank loan agreements, bills of installment sales, insurance policies, and leases, have brought storms of protest from lawyers who hold that ancient phraseology has been interpreted by many courts.

Lawyers fear plain language would be legally ambiguous and, as a result, would discourage corporations from operating in a particular state. (It might also, perhaps, reduce the need for lawyers.)

The New York State law requires that "every written agreement" involving sums of money, goods, or services valued at $50,000 or less be "written in" nontechnical language and in a clear and coherent manner using words with common and everyday meanings. A Washington attorney responds with: "Simple language is great for consumer brochures or explanation of bills, but you can't expect an industry to operate under third-grade English when the penalty is whopping fines."

NEW WORDS

In every era there are words created to express a hybrid or a new concept. Made words are not a contemporary phenomenon: All of our vocabulary was new at one time. But in a time of new and changing concepts, new words—called neologisms—proliferate, and learning to use them will add a dimension and flavor to your language.

A large group of new words are conceived by compounding or by adding prefixes or suffixes. Thus, brinkmanship, one-upmanship, showmanship, antihero, antiestablishment, antiintellectual; cinemactress, cinerama, telethon, talkathon.

Another form of adapting language is to invent word forms of your own for a special situation. From John Steinbeck, we quote:

Let me say in the beginning that even if I wanted to avoid Texas I could not, for I am lawed in Texas, and mother-in-lawed, and uncled, and aunted, and cousined within an inch of my life.

Renowned as a word maker, particularly of portmanteau words, was Walter Winchell, Broadway gossip columnist, who invented "infanticipating," "cigargoyle," and "featherwit." These nonce words serve to meet a one-time situation. But it is not a Winchell monopoly. James Joyce used "bisexcycle." Lewis Carroll's "slithy" is made up of slimy and lithe, and "snizzle" is a compound of snow and drizzle. Others are "seething eye dog," "Castrocize," "front-tier belle."

Snobography—getting the right seat at the right restaurant.
—Burt Boyer, *Esquire,* January 1962

Queuemania is an ailment that afflicts people with a compulsive urge to line up behind someone or something, even a lamp-post.
—Thomas P. Ronan

A waiter with a provocatip smile.
—Morris Bender, *Reader's Digest*

Monopologues are his specialty.

Dentopedalogy is the science of opening your mouth and putting your foot in it. I've been practicing it for years.
—Philip, Duke of Edinburgh, to Britain's General Dental Council

A vice-president in an advertising agency is a "molehill man." A molehill man is a pseudo-busy executive who comes to work at 9 a.m. and finds a molehill on his desk. He has until 5 p.m. to make this molehill into a mountain. An accomplished molehill man will often have his mountain finished even before lunch.
—Fred Allen

The Republicans have a "me too" candidate running on a "yes but" platform, advised by a "has been" staff.
—Adlai Stevenson

Acronyms become words, especially when the institutions or elements they represent are long or complicated: UNESCO, NATO, LOX (liquid oxygen explosive), laser (light amplification by stimulated emission of radiation).

Some "new words" creating new concepts in public affairs become part of history:

We are in the midst of a *cold war* . . .

—Bernard Baruch, 1948

There is here [in America] a great *melting pot* in which we must compound a precious metal. That metal is the metal of nationality.

—Woodrow Wilson, 1915

I am looking forward to a continuation . . . of the policy that will work for the good of the average citizen in the United States, that will not forget the *forgotten man*.

—Franklin D. Roosevelt, 1936

We shall not, I believe, be obliged to alter our policy of *watchful waiting*.

We stand today on the edge of a *new frontier*—the frontier of the 1960's—a frontier of unknown opportunities and perils—a frontier of unfulfilled hopes and threats.

—John F. Kennedy, 1960

In the field of world policy, I would dedicate this nation to the policy of the *good neighbor*.

—Franklin D. Roosevelt, 1933

. . . with all deliberate speed . . .

—U.S. Supreme Court order, in a decision ordering desegregation, 1955

One of our defects as a nation is a tendency to use what have been called "weasel words." When a weasel sucks eggs the meat is sucked out of the egg. If you use a "weasel word" after another there is nothing left of the other.

—Theodore Roosevelt

And from a news report on the Russian taxi driver:

The cabbie invariably responds with what one American wag has called *the primal stare,* a vacant mixture of loathing and non-comprehension that is the master tool of the bureaucrat.

—*The New York Times,* April 25, 1977

THE ARCHAIC

Archaic words are usually used to create an authentic background for a historical novel, but they may also lend an exotic element to contemporary expression. Legal documents make much use of "hereinafter," "aforesaid," "hereby." When you wish to create an elevated effect, to coin an epigram with dignity of instant age, to borrow dignity, you may find archaic expressions appropriate.

The archaic flavor is sometimes useful because it suggests the authority of the Bible, or at least of tradition and age.

He that multiplieth the doers is greater than he that doeth the work.

—John B. Mott

In George Bernard Shaw's play *How He Lied to Her Husband,* a young man of eighteen justifies his feelings for a woman of thirty-seven:

Perfect love casteth off fear.

And this is a common expression:

His cup runneth over.

You may achieve certain poetic effects by using archaic language:

Whence are thy beams, O sun! thy everlasting light? Thou comest forth, in thy awful beauty; the stars hide themselves in the sky; the moon, cold and pale, sinks in the western wave. But thou, thyself movest alone.

—James MacPherson

COLLOQUIAL LANGUAGE

Often you'll discover that using colloquial language is particularly helpful in establishing a rapport with your audience.

This is no time for quitters or for a lot of talk about instant surrender. I don't think the American people want to clamber aboard some sort of bugout shuttle.

—Melvin R. Laird

I have no expectation of making a hit every time I come to bat.

—Franklin D. Roosevelt, 1933

They've been peddling eyewash about themselves and hogwash about Democrats. What they need is a good mouthwash.

—Senator Lyndon B. Johnson

The buck stops here.

—Sign on President Harry S Truman's desk

It has been presented to us as a program of more for our money —national security in the large economy size package—a bigger bang for a buck.

—Adlai Stevenson

No nation likes noise and "Hooey" like we do. We are cuckoo but happy.

—Will Rogers

Nice guys finish last.

—Leo Durocher

When the crowd shouted: "Give 'em hell, Harry!", Truman remarked: "I never give them hell. I just tell the truth, and they think it is hell."

SLANG

Slang is useful in avoiding the dull familiarity of conservative language, in personalizing a statement, or in bringing the statement into everyday reality. At times, the introduction of slang in a context of standard language serves as a stopper, an attention grabber. In addition, the use of slang characterizes the speaker as down-to-earth, forceful, acceptable. Overall, the use of slang can produce a pleasing bit of prose.

> There's a sucker born every minute.
> —Phineas T. Barnum

> Hello sucker!
> —Texas Guinan, nightclub hostess, 1920

> Nuts!
> —Reply of Major General Anthony C. McAuliffe
> in response to a German demand for surrender
> at Bastogne, Belgium, December 22, 1944

An interesting use of slang is presented in O. Henry's story "By Courier."

A message is given:

> Tell her I am on my way to the station, to leave for San Francisco, where I shall join that Alaska moosehunting expedition. Tell her that, since she has commanded me neither to speak nor to write to her, I take this means of making one last appeal to her sense of justice, for the sake of what has been. Tell her that to condemn and discard one who has not deserved such treatment, without giving him her reason or a chance to explain is contrary to her nature as I believe it to be.

The message is delivered:

> He told me to tell yer he's got his collars and cuffs in dat grip for a scoot clean out to 'Frisco. Den he's goin' to shoot snowbirds in de Klondike. He says yer told him to send 'round no more pink notes nor come hangin' over de garden gate, and he takes dis means (sending the boy to speak for him, that is) of putting yer wise. He says yer referred to him like a has-been, and never give him no chance to kick at de decision. He says yer swiled him and never said why.

Charles Dickens builds a scene with slang in the dialogue:

"Never mind," said the stranger, cutting the address very short, "said enough—no more; smart chap that cabman—handled his fives well; but if I'd been your friend in the green jemmy—damn me—punch his head,—God I would—pig's whisper—pieman too,—no gammon."
This coherent speech was interrupted by the entrance of the Rochester coachman, to announce that . . .

—Charles Dickens, *Pickwick Papers*

In the political arena, you can usually use slang effectively:

No matter how thin you slice it, it's still baloney.

—Alfred E. Smith

Practical uses? Here are some advertisements:

Gutsy Lady.

—Van Raalte

What's happened to America's Genius for The Watchamacallit, The Doohickey, The Gismo?

—CBS Radio Network

Which one is The Top Honcho?

—*Dun's Review*

JARGON

Jargon is the language of a special group. It usually consists of old words given new meanings—a sort of code. Thus, in underworld jargon, "dolls" are girls, "H" is heroin, "bag-man" is the receiver of illicit money. Often these expressions flow into the general vocabulary and into colloquial usage. Humbug, bluff, OK, sham, skim, once part of a private language, are now widely accepted. Unless they become clichés, such colorful words can add sparkle to your phrases.

Here is an example of the use of eighteenth-century jargon in Byron's *Don Juan*:

> He from the world had cut off a great man,
> Who in his time had made heroic bustle.
> Who in a row like Tom could lead the van,
> Booze in the ken [1], or at the spellken [2] hustle?

> Who queer a flat [3]? Who (spite of Bow street's ban)
> On the high toby-spice [4] so flash the muzzle?
> Who on a lark [5], with black-eyed Sal (his blowing)[6]
> So prime, so swell [7], so nutty [8], and so knowing?

It requires this illumination:

[1] ken = a house which harbors thieves
[2] spellken = a playhouse or theatre
[3] to queer a flat = to puzzle a silly fellow
[4] to flash the muzzle (gun) on the high toby-spice = to rob on horseback
[5] a lark = fun or sport of any kind
[6] a blowing = a girl
[7] swell = gentlemanly
[8] nutty = pleasing (to be nuts on = to be infatuated with)

Byron afterward commented ironically:

The advance of science and of language has rendered it unnecessary to translate the above good and true English, spoken in its original purity by the select nobility and their patrons. The following is a stanza of a song which was very popular, at least in my early days:—

> On the high toby-spice flash the muzzle,
> In spite of each gallows old scout;
> If you at all spellken can't hustle,
> You'll be hobbled in making a clout.
> Then your Blowing will wax gallows haughty,
> When she hears of your scaly mistake,
> She'll surely turn snitch for the forty—
> That her Jack may be regular weight.

Damon Runyon was a master at jargon. This is from "Old Em's Kentucky Home":

All this really begins the April day at the Jamaica race track when an assistant starter by the name of Plumbuff puts a twitch on Itchky Ironhat's fourteen-year-old race mare, Emaleen, who is known to one and all as Em for short.

A twitch is nothing but a rope loop that they wrap around a horse's upper lip and keep twisting with a stick to make the horse stand quiet at the starting gate and while I never have a twitch on my own lip and hope and trust that I never have same, I do not see anything wrong with putting twitches on horses' lips, especially the ones I am betting against as it generally keeps them so busy thinking of how it hurts that they sometimes forget about running.

However, it seems that Itchky Ironhat not only considers a twitch very painful to horses, but he also considers it undignified for such a horse as old Em, because while every body regards Em as strictly a porcupine Itchky thinks she is the best horse in the world and loves her so dearly he cannot bear to see her in pain or made to look undignified. To tell the truth, it is common gossip that Itchky loves old Em more than he loves anything else, whatever, including his ever-loving wife, Mousie.

DIALECT

Dialectal language—the borrowing of foreign expressions —has a much wider use than most of us immediately appreciate. The use of dialect in humor is a common device. Like jargon, slang, and colloquial language, dialect words provide a time and place setting, an indication of your background or the background of your fictional characters.

Barbaralexis or *barbarismus* from the Greek "foreign mode of speech," which we call dialect, was commonly used in literature from earliest times. It is usually frowned upon in public speaking today as offensive to ethnic minorities. It can be used, however, to establish a rapport with a special group and is almost always used humorously.

They say a reasonable number of fleas is good fer a dog—keeps him from broodin' over bein' a dog.
—Edward N. Westcott, *David Harum*, 1898

In literary works, you may utilize dialect for purposes of characterization. This is from John Galsworthy's "A Bit of Love."

Mrs. Burlacomble: Zurely! I give 'im a nummit afore 'e gets up; an' 'e 'as 'is brekjus reg'lar at nine. Must feed un up. He'm on 'is feet all day, goin' to zee folk that widden want to zee an angel,

they'm that busy; an' when 'e comes in 'e 'll play 'is flute there.
He'm wastin' away for want of 'is wife. That's what 'tis. On' 'im
so zweet-spoken, tu, 'tis a pleasure to year 'im—Never zays a
word!

Mixing two languages can have a witty effect. Here, Latin
is combined with English:

Harricum! Harricum! Give 'em hell Harricum!
—Oxford University cheer for Harry S Truman

VULGARISMS

Another form of nonstandard vocabulary involves the use
of vulgarisms. Although once shocking, much of this has now
become acceptable in everyday oral communication. But in
writing there is still a prudishness that follows the formula
of the transcripts of the Watergate tapes: "expletive deleted."
Expletives are intensified interjections and they find their
way into novels today as they did in the sixteenth century.
They are coarse, with a high emotional charge, and serve to
express these emotions.

A more acceptable variation is a combination of solecisms,
colloquialisms, foreign expressions, and grammatical irrever-
ences:

No matter whether th' constitution follows th' flag or not, th'
supreme court follows th' iliction returns.
—Finley Peter Dunne

Nobuddy ever fergits where he buried a hatchet.
—Kin Hubbard

Hit 'em where they ain't.
—Willie Keeler, great baseball placement hitter

Git thar fustest with the mostest.
—Erroneous version of Nathan Bedford Forrest's
statement, reported by Generals Duke and Taylor

Nobody can't never get nothing for nothing nowhere, no time,
nohow.

HUMOR

As a device in communication, humor is much more than a figure or a scheme: It is a whole approach that can have magical powers, even surpassing those of the rhetoric of the ancients. Humor can change an antagonistic or neutral audience into a receptive, friendly group of listeners in a few minutes. In this way, it performs a major function in communication in creating acceptance of what follows. It breaks down barriers between strangers, allays suspicion, makes friends with a single joining in laughter. Basically, it gets the audience on your side. "Only the emotion of love rates higher rank [in giving pleasure] than the emotion of laughter," Max Beerbohm estimates.

All of us know that most speeches made outside of academia—and many within it—begin with a "story," a relaxer to get the audience to listen favorably, to accept the speaker as a hail-fellow. In the 1976 presidential campaign, there were a few such attempts. The standard Ronald Reagan speech was no Gettysburg address, but it lit up the audience. Sample warm-up joke:

> A man in traction in a hospital pays no attention to the visitor bending anxiously over him. Finally, the patient opens his eyes and explains in a discreet Irish brogue that he kept silent because he wanted to savor the moment: "It's been six months here since I've had a drink, and your breath is like the rain from heaven."

With a few laughs under his belt, Reagan launched his attack on "Big Government." A favorite line is one he used in the Barry Goldwater campaign in 1964: "A Government bureau is the nearest thing to eternal life that we'll ever see on this earth."

The nearly constant element in the speeches along the vice-presidential campaign trail during the same period was a joke without a point. The press called it "the bear story." It was told by candidate Robert Dole nineteen times in one month:

> A bear, it seems, walked into a bar, ordered a bottle of beer and put a five dollar bill on the counter. The bartender served the bear, then rushed to his back room boss for instructions. "Give it back a nickel," said the boss. "It will never know the difference."
>
> Some time later the bartender, fascinated, walked around and took a stool next to his new customer. "You know," the bartender said, "we don't have many bears in here." The bear replied, "I don't suppose you do at $4.95 a drink."

"Now there's a moral to that story," Mr. Dole told a St. Louis fund-raising dinner, "and we're working on it, and if you have any suggestions, send them to Jimmy Carter's headquarters in Peanutville, America."

As we know, however, humor also has a venomous side. While getting a laugh, you can ridicule a person or an issue into oblivion or raise it into prominence. The magazine *Punch,* with its humor, did much to change the way of law and life in the British Empire, and the cartoonist remains a prominent part of the world press.

What then, makes something funny? How can you use humor to your advantage? The subject has been drawn and quartered for centuries.

Humor—and comedy, a close cousin—are extremely personal things. Submit a score of "humorous" stories to a score of people and each will find a different half dozen the funniest. In fact, the French writer Marcel Pagnol once noted that the source of laughter was not in funny things or situations themselves, but in the background of the one who laughs.

Literature is full of essays that try to figure out what makes something funny. Writes E. B. White: "Analysts have had their go at humor but without being greatly instructed." Freud relates the comic to dreams. Humor can be dissected, as a frog can, but the thing dies in the process. Humor proves to be a fragile, evasive thing until the audience has become conditioned to expect the next words to be funny. Then the audience can become hysterical, uncontrollable.

WHAT MAKES IT FUNNY

For all its evanescence, humor in the contemporary age has several distinct elements upon which you can draw for oral or written needs:

You can provide an unexpected finale. The suddenness of the transition, the alternation of tears and laughter, the balking of expectations are key elements.

The eccentric five-year old son of an affluent family was spoiled; and with the purchase of a motor-driven hobbyhorse his odd behavior became bizarre. He refused to leave the saddle, taking his meals there and sleeping in an upright position. Family doctors were unable to budge him. In desperation a psychologist was called. The specialist put a fatherly hand on the boy's shoulder, whispered gently into his ear, and the boy leaped from the horse.

After the fee was paid and the family was alone the boy's mother said, "You refused to obey the doctors, me, your father, or your tutors. What did the man say that made you obey?"

The boy refused to divulge the information unless he was promised a new motorboat. A check was drawn, placed in his hand, and again the mother asked:

"Now, what did he say?"

"Well, mother," the child confided, "He said, 'get the hell off that lousy horse or I'll break every bone in your body.' "

—Gerald F. Lieberman, *The Greatest Laughs of All Time*

You can make a direct inference that, in some way, a character is ridiculous, that the people in the audience are superior to the victim. To do this you may expose a human frailty or imperfection—especially the failure of one in high esteem. Or superiority may flow from some special knowledge the audience has which the character does not have. The success of "Polish" or "dialect" jokes, or of the circumlocutionary art of Milt Gross are illustrative. Superiority massages the ego—and thus exposes the malice in all of us. Hypocrisy, affectation, pretense are its targets.

Your audience will delight in a teacher's error (or even a student's), the exposure of a sin in the sanctimonious, the exposure of two faces of a politician, the destruction of an idol, even a preacher sneezing, the die-hard overturned, the cuckold, the puritan ensnared, the failings of hierarchy, the eloquent speaker with a toothache, the person giving the impression of being a mechanical thing—a puppet, a jack-in-the-box—stuttering, lisping, foreign accents. These are elements out of which your humor may be created. Humor says: "The absurdity of it." Your readers or listeners thus purge themselves of an underlying sense of inferiority in the embarrassment of others.

An orderly in a hospital for the mentally disturbed reported that one of the inmates had escaped. "Got away, huh?" the chief neurologist asked. "Did you guard all the exits?"

"I did," said the orderly. "He must have left by one of the entrances."

—Gerald F. Lieberman, *The Greatest Laughs of All Time*

So much in life is absurd that there is scarcely any limitation on what you can use to provoke laughter. But there are areas that are especially fertile for humor. As we have already suggested, any affectation or failing is a likely target: vanity, hypocrisy, prejudice, superstition, ignorance—in fact any difference from our own accepted morals. Enthusiasm about trifles and devotion to nonsense hold a special place in our sensitivity.

When prejudice, whim, and caprice are consistent and absurd, the humor flows smoothly and naturally. Your readers or listeners will laugh at the unreasonable and the unnecessary: The credo that the man in the family makes all the decisions, that the husband proposes to his wife (not vice versa), that mothers-in-law are interfering, that all uncles are rich, all these elements provide you with good material for laughter. This is true also of social precedence, protocol, manners in general, diehards, those who think they are what they are not, situations that are not what they are supposed to be. Excessive impudence, excessive modesty—in fact excess of any characteristic is good soil for humor.

Our ridicule builds on certain supposed (or accepted) information, whether it is true or false, and on what we consider to be right, whether it is right or wrong. So build your humor on the prejudices of your audience, in contrast with the "ridiculous" prejudices of others. Thus it will touch some experience in your listeners or readers.

Laughter will also flow when you interject the incongruous, the non sequitur, the disconnecting of one idea from another, the jostling of one feeling against another. A laugh bursts out when you describe an unexpected misstep, even if it is not ludicrous, although a victim may not always consider it funny. The event you depict becomes ludicrous where the contradiction is the more-than-usually-unexpected—as when the mistake is made by an expert. Your skill with humor increases with the degree of unexpectedness you provide.

"This is a simple test to determine ordinary response," the psychiatrist told his patient.

"What would happen if I cut off your left ear?"

"I couldn't hear."

"And what would happen if I then cut off your right ear?"

"I couldn't see."

"Why?"

"My hat would fall over my eyes."

Exaggeration in anecdote—even sheer lying—is another way you can create amusement. The stories of Baron Munchausen are classics:

THE AUTHENTIC ADVENTURE OF BARON MUNCHAUSEN AND HIS GLORIOUS HORSE

The swiftness of my Lithuanian enabled me to be foremost in the pursuit; and seeing the enemy fairly flying through the opposite gate, I thought it would be prudent to stop in the marketplace, to order the men to rendezvous. I stopped, gentlemen; but judge of my astonishment when in this marketplace I saw not one of my hussars about me. Are they scouring the other streets? Or what is become of them? They could not be far off, and must, at all events, soon join me. In that expectation I walked my panting Lithuanian to a spring in this marketplace, and let him drink. He drank uncommonly, with an eagerness not to be satisfied, but natural enough; for when I looked around for my men, what should I see, gentlemen! the hind part of the poor creature—croup and legs were missing, as if he had been cut in two, and the water ran out as it came in, without refreshing or doing him any good! How it could have happened was quite a mystery to me, till I returned with him to the towngate. There I saw, that when I rushed in pell-mell with the flying enemy, they had dropped the portcullis [a heavy falling door, with sharp spikes at the bottom, let down suddenly to prevent the entrance of an enemy into a fortified town] unperceived by me, which had totally cut off his hind part, that still lay quivering on the outside of the gate.

Misunderstanding can be funny. You might play on the difference in perception when two people are talking about different things or in a different context (Abbott & Costello's "Who's on first") or when one party in the dialogue is unaware of some circumstance or of what the other thinks of him. In such cases, you can make the conversation purposefully ambiguous and the statements equivocal.

At the doctor's office she needed only one general question and was off on a two-hour dissertation of her troubles. "You know something," she finally said, "You're wonderful. When I came in here I had a headache, but it's disappeared." "You are wrong, madam," replied the psychiatrist. "I have it now."

This is from an 1871 collection, the *New London Jest Book*:

An innocent lad one evening went up to the drawing room on the bell being rung. When he returned to the kitchen, he laughed immoderately. Some of the servants asking the cause of his mirth, he cried, "What do you think. There are sixteen of them who could not snuff the candles and were obliged to send for me."

Humor is easily created if you invent a character who is consistently absurd or is devoted to a cause that is incongruous with his personality. Comic cartoonists make much of this by attributing a set personality to their characters. The effect is often cumulative, as one absurdity is piled on another. The dumb student was a favorite butt:

"How many wars did we fight with Spain?" the professor asked the gridiron flash.
"Seven."
"Seven, hey? Can you enumerate them?"
"Certainly," the athlete replied. "One, two, three, four, five, six, seven."

—Gerald F. Lieberman, *The Greatest Laughs of All Time*

Similarly, if you show someone acting out of character you'll get a laugh. For example, you might describe a situation in which a child teaches a parent or lectures a minister. Humor itself is a distortion, but it should not be an unpleasant distortion.

It was a romantic, moonlit night filled with the perfume of lilacs. Finally he got up the courage to ask: "What will make you mine forever?"

Sweetly, she replied: "A five carat diamond ring, darling."

Anything that the mind is forbidden to think about is ripe for laughter: the private joke, a wanton wisecrack (especially in times when sex was still a forbidden area of polite conversation). Wickedness has often been a substitute for wit. "It is the nature of comedy to be erotic, risqué or sensuous if not sensual, impious and even wicked" one critic, Suzanne Langer, observes. "It is easier to stimulate an audience by direct stimulation of feeling and fantasy, not by an artistic power."

A New Yorker was about to check in at the Caracas Hilton when he saw a beautiful Venezuelan girl sitting in the lobby. He introduced himself to her politely and then checked in with her as Mr. and Mrs. Smith. The next morning when he checked out, the cashier gave him a bill for $865. The guy screamed, "$865—I was only here one night!"

The clerk said, "I know—but your wife has been here for six months."

—Joey Adams

You can obtain a humorous effect by transposing the natural expression of an idea into another key—transposing the solemn into the familiar, or parodying something. Humor comes from something being out of context. When Sid Caesar and Imogene Coca "sang" grand opera on the old *Show of Shows*, they carried the serious into the realm of the hilarious.

Your audience will laugh at the grotesque, yet not at the distorted body, a limping man. But the person who acts mechanically *is* funny. There is a fine line that you must not cross in attempting to amuse. A mildly stupid character can be amusing, but a mentally retarded person is regarded as tragic. A hypochondriac is funny but a sick man is not. Your audience will laugh at disappointment in trifles, but cry at what thwarts their needs in serious matters.

When your readers or listeners are in a happy state almost

anything seems funny. An audience conditioned to laughter expecting to laugh—will respond to your every word and gesture. If your audience knows in advance that you will provide comedy, they will be preconditioned to accept humor —and are thus more easily roused by it. The audience laughs at the recollection of having laughed, at the expectation of laughing, and even at just the appearance of the person expected to make them laugh. Once you have established a pattern of laughter, repeating a key word may release a repressed feeling in your audience that goes off like a spring.

WHO WILL LAUGH?

Because laughter is contagious, each subsequent laugh is easier to stimulate than the one before. However, you cannot force people to laugh. Not everyone will laugh because he is expected to laugh, and when the humor does not strike a chord in a reader or listener, it elicits a response like: "I don't see anything funny about that." People are conditioned by long experience before they meet your particular brand of humor. What is drastically unexpected by one person is less unexpected by another.

A serious mood in the audience, as in a time when a problem faces the community or some members of the audience, makes it more difficult for you to elicit laughter. (A good, relevant story will help break the mood.)

Sometimes your audience may think it should not laugh —because it thinks your type of comedy is obscene, because you are speaking or writing as a political opponent or a rival, and so forth. This restraint often makes the temptation to laugh even greater. The longer you can make the audience hold that impulse in restraint, the more violent is its final release. As a speaker, you can adapt your words to the changing mood of the audience. As a writer, the audience is particularly a challenge. You cannot "feel" their mood. You must "select" your audience or condition it to fit the mood of the humor.

CHAPTER

WIT

Freud distinguished comedy, humor, and wit in this way:

> The pleasure of wit originates from an economy of expenditure in exhibition, of the comic from an economy of expenditure in thought, and of humor from an economy of expenditure in feeling.

Comedy is humor that is impersonal and polite, like a smile. Wit is a child of humor, but it has many singular facets. It often makes no friends, and frequently it makes enemies. In action, it is the cutting edge of humor, for better or worse. Geoffrey Bocca commented:

> Wit is a treacherous dart. It is perhaps the only weapon with which it is possible to stab one's self in one's own back.

Wit, of course, is not an organized system in itself. It utilizes rhetorical devices, most of which have already been discussed, relying principally on the perception of similarities in dissimilar things, on parallels, and on contrasts. Situations or semantics are its material. It plays on words and ideas, involving many of the devices of rhetoric: the pun, alliteration, onomatopoeia, the schemes, oxymoron (the paradox), metathesis (transposition of letters), zeugma (using a verb with different senses in the same sentence), syncrisis (comparing contrary elements in contrasting sentences), fable, hypotyposis (mimicry of acts), mimesis (mimicry of word or gesture), aenos (quoting fables)—almost the whole galaxy of rhetoric is at your command when you are dealing with wit.

The etymological ancestors of the word *wit* have much to do with intelligence. The word itself derives from the Old English *witan*, to know. The *witenagemot* (a meeting of wise men) was the first parliamentary body in England. Even now we use the expressions "to be at wits' end," "to lose one's wits," "half-wit," "nitwit," "dimwit," etc. Thus, for more than a thousand years, "wit" has signified in the English language "mind," "intellect," "intelligence."

Notwithstanding its importance, wit was never clearly delimited. Although for most of history it was identified with intellect, in its heyday it was the force that defied a definition but was generally well understood. At the beginning of the sixteenth century, "wit" merged with two ancient traditions—rhetoric and psychology. Thereafter for more than a hundred years, from about 1650 to 1750, its meaning was enriched to meet the needs of an era recorded by some as "The Age of Wit."

Anyone of intellect during this period prided himself on his displays of wit as criticism, satire, or raillery. Ben Jonson had earlier laid the groundwork with skilled satire. John Dryden was a master of satire at the end of the seventeenth century.

> Wits now arrived to a more high degree;
> Our native language more refined and full;
> Our ladies and our men now speak more wit.
> In conversation, than those poets writ.
> —John Dryden

"THE REPUBLIC OF LETTERS"

At this time there was a revitalization of "the republic of letters," a sort of association of wits with a code of ethics for

the community of cultivated minds made up of poets, drama-
tists, and other writers. Wit then became a balance of judgment
and imagination—an exhibition of mental adroitness ex-
hibited in rhetorical display. The established leaders considered themselves bound to use their talents for the public
good. (But in practice wit often stooped to private ends for
compensation of one sort or another.) The philosophy was
based on Aeschylus's precept:

> . . . we, the poets, are teachers of men. We are things honest
> and pure to speak.

The dedication to good was of short duration, limited by
varying ideas and considerations of what was "good" and by
the same human frailties we know today.

During a hundred years, this wit was a major force in everyday living and in literature, and indeed, in the whole fabric of
social life. It dominated and saturated conversations at coffee-
house and court. It became an intellectual force that stimulated or stifled social progress. In a sense, it was the hallmark
of the late seventeenth and the eighteenth century—of the
Augustan Age, when John Dryden, Alexander Pope, Jonathan
Swift, Samuel Johnson, and Daniel Defoe were some of the
luminaries of the day.

Wit was used to enlighten, to denigrate, to display the intellect, and to provide enjoyment. Thomas Burke, the historian,
puts it this way: "Men and women were rude in a more elegant
way; they said lewd things with a finer accent, and kicked citizens with a touch of polish."

In the affluent and intellectually dynamic period after the
restoration of Charles II to the throne in 1660, alive with many
great intellects and much urbanity, there were ample stimulants
for wit to flourish, although it was, at the same time, a period
with much to deplore: filth and plague, starvation and crime,
profligate immorality. But there was enough wealth to allow
an opportunity for a wit to earn a living, usually under the
auspices of someone of wealth or power.

WHAT IS WIT?

How then do you achieve wit? As all humor, wit contains an element of surprise and invention, but it is more dependent on aptness and enigma. You have to strike a balance so that your wit is not too obvious, yet not too difficult to grasp either. To meet its practical problems, wit involves a basic formula. You must provide an element of perplexity—the meaning must not be too quickly apparent. (A common story is the example of the man who began to laugh in church on Sunday at a witty comment he had heard Saturday night.)

Wit uses one or more of the techniques of rhetoric, and you can choose from a galaxy of devices and ornaments varying from the metaphor to exhortation. It is supposed to present the truth, and it depends on at least the half truth, but it operates as effectively to distort, confuse, or obfuscate the truth. And to be pungent it should have a subtle effect upon the ego or other areas of sensitivity common to all of us. It utilizes exaggeration of a part or the whole (caricature).

Wit is essentially the "eloquence of indifference" as William Hazlitt defined it, "an ingenious and striking exposition of those glancing impressions of objects which affect us more from surprise or contrast to the train of our ordinary and literal preconceptions, than from anything in the objects themselves exciting our necessary sympathy or lasting hatred." It adds littleness to littleness, exposing humor by comparing a situation or contrasting it with the expected. It is not merely a wisecrack or a sarcastic remark. "Wit has truth in it; wisecracking is simply calisthenics with words," Dorothy Parker said.

SATIRE

Satire is the knife in the armory of wit. It is usually characterized as venomous, cutting, stinging. The laughter of satire is a blow on the back or in the face. But in a sense, satire is an aggressive form of flattery, an imitation fired by indignation. In the tradition of "I don't care what you say about me as long as you spell my name right," satire attaches importance to what it deplores.

Aristotle noted two kinds of poets—those who produce hymns and panegyrics and those who produce "envectures"—satires, lampoons. These were generally written in an iambic meter, which soon made "iambs" synonymous with invective.

The word satire itself—from the Latin *satura* ("full")—develops into the meaning "a mixture of different things." For a time satire was erroneously associated with the Greek Satyr, the "base god being conversant with man's affairs, and who spies out all their secret faults." Thus satire is rude, licentious, bold, harsh, rough: "Like the porcupine that shoots sharpe quills out in each angry line and wounds the blushing cheeks, and fiery eye, of him that hears, and readeth guiltily," said the rhetorician George Puttenham. Satire was so dangerous in the golden era of Greek literature that Plato proposed to ban ridicule entirely from the ideal state.

For the effect on an audience, you as a satirist must rely heavily on subliminal feelings of guilt or shame. Most people —primitive or sophisticated—are conditioned by training to feel guilt strongly for many deeds or thoughts. Almost everyone is pained by the thought that neighbors are laughing at him. The power of ridicule has indeed changed the course of history. Today, the great lampoon events are the annual American press banquets, such as the one in Washington, D.C., of the Gridiron Club, the association of fifty newspaper correspondents. Traditionally, similar events are held in state capitals and in New York City—by political and financial organizations.

Inasmuch as these lampoons are "off the record"—not to be reported in the press—public figures accept the ridicule gracefully. They have little choice other than to further publicize the commentary and to be considered spoilsports. But when it goes on to publication, the ridicule brings with it shame, the fear of contempt, abandonment, "death by emotional starvation," even for the mightiest. In the modern world ridicule remains a prime force for enforcing conformity.

The areas of humor in wit are extensive but the essence is found in the techniques of "put-down"—cynicism, iconoclasm, retort, one-upmanship, etc.

THE PUT-DOWN

The "put-down"—the critic's power to comment on man and his work—is basic satire. The Greeks had a term *tapinosis*, meaning "reduction or humiliation," the Romans called it *humilatio*, and Puttenham named it *abbaser*. Peacham says this device is used "when the majesty of a high matter is brought down" and gave as an example calling a musician a fiddler. Modern writers are more devastating. Here's how some modern writers express themselves.

In less inspired moments she followed the music as a bear might pursue a mouse.
                    —Adrian Stokes, *Tonight the Ballet*

Katharine Hepburn ran the whole gamut of emotions, from A to B.
                                        —Dorothy Parker

Tallulah Bankhead barged down the Nile last week as Cleopatra—and sank.
                    —John Mason Brown, reviewing
                       Antony and Cleopatra

Winston Churchill was a master at it. In the House of Commons, commenting on a remark by George Wyndham, a member of Parliament, he said:

If I valued the honourable gentleman's opinion I might get angry.

And from another prime minister:

> Mr. Kremlin was distinguished for ignorance; for he had only one idea—and that was wrong.
>
> —Benjamin Disraeli

And from a professional critic:

> This man was hired to depress art. This is the opinion of Will Blake.
>
> —William Blake, *of Sir Joshua Reynolds*

> The dogs were poorly supported by the rest of the cast.
>
> —Don Herold, review of *Uncle Tom's Cabin*

> She loves nature—in spite of what it did to her.

> He gives the kind of performance that gives failure a bad name.

THE RETORT

In an era when one-upmanship is accepted almost as part of the social fabric, the quick retort is a test of wit. The need to reply quickly and well may occur anytime. Winston Churchill was renowned for his responses—especially under fire.

The American-born Lady Nancy Astor entered Parliament as its first woman member. During the appeasement period preceding World War II, Lady Astor was a weekend guest at Blenheim and exchanged barbs with Churchill.

> Lady Astor: "Winston, if I were your wife, I'd put poison in your coffee."
>
> W.S.C.: "If I were your husband, Nancy, I'd take it."

When it was demanded of a newspaper to retract a statement it had printed saying, "Half of the city officials are crooks," they retracted with, "Half of the city officials aren't crooks."

On his birthday, a rabbi received a picture of a pig as a present. He sent back a photograph of himself, inscribed, "You sent me a picture of yourself, I send you mine."

When asked, "Who was your father?" Alexander Dumas responded: "My father was a creole, his father a Negro, and his father a monkey; my family, it seems, begins where yours left off."

Governor Giles of Virginia wrote to Patrick Henry demanding satisfaction:

Sir, I understand that you have called me a "bob-tail" politician. I wish to know if it be true; and if true, your meaning.

Mr. Henry responded:

Sir, I do not recollect having called you a bob-tail politician at any time but I think probably I have. Not recollecting the time or occasion I can't say what I meant, but if you will tell me what you think I meant, I will say whether you are correct.

To a heckler:

If you're ever in California, sir, I do hope you'll come by and use my pool—I'd love to give you some drowning lessons!
—Sammy Davis, Jr.

A famous exchange of insults went thus:

Gladstone: "You sir, will die either on the gallows or of some loathsome disease."
Disraeli: "That sir, depends upon whether I embrace your principles or your mistress."

My opponent wraps himself up in the flimsy garment of his own righteousness and then complains of the cold.
—Winston Churchill

CYNICISM

There is something in cynicism, a less caustic form of sarcasm, which in itself smacks of personal superiority and conveys it to the audience. You have only to point out some frailty to seem to become superior to it. Attributing that frailty to an individual presumably makes you superior to that individual.

Cynicism is always in fashion. The Greek Cynics, led by Antisthenes (444 B.C.), believed that virtue was the only good, and that it was attained through self-control and independence. Their modern counterparts believe that virtue does not exist, that all actions are motivated by self-interest, and thus they expect the worst from everyone—and see all actions as selfishly motivated, all rules as subject to evasion, and all statements as self-serving. This iconoclastic viewpoint, breaking down the values set by society, is a pose you must assume for successful cynicism. In a sense, as a cynic you have to belittle continually—but often you can do so with a sense of humor. This is how some writers have used it effectively:

Burgoyne: Martyrdom . . . is the only way in which a man can become famous without ability.
—George Bernard Shaw, *The Devil's Disciple*

After you lose your membership in it, the younger generation seems pretty bad.
—*Baptist and Reflector,* Nashville, Tenn.

Woman's virtue is man's greatest invention.
—Cornelia Otis Skinner

I guess Prohibition is better than no liquor at all.
—Will Rogers

Nothing so needs reforming as other people's habits.
—Mark Twain

Talk to a man about himself and he will listen for hours.
—Benjamin Disraeli

An alcoholic is someone who drinks too much—and you don't like anyway.

The most difficult secret for a man to keep is his own opinion of himself.

—Marcel Pagnol

Many people consider the things government does for them to be social progress—but they consider the things government does for others as socialism.

—Earl Wilson

You ask me to read you my epigrams. No thank you—you want to read me yours, not to hear mine!

—Martial

When a fellow says, "It ain't the money but the principle o' the thing," it's th' money.

—Kin Hubbard

He that falls in love with himself will have no rivals.

—Benjamin Franklin

Man is the only animal that blushes. Or needs to.

—Mark Twain

Opera is when a guy gets stabbed in the back and instead of bleeding he sings.

—Ed Gardner

A true friend is one who likes you despite your achievements.

Most of today's families are broke. It will just take a depression to make it official.

—Gregory Nunn

It's a wonderful generation to belong to. Everything that's wrong is the fault of the generation ahead of us and is going to have to be corrected by the one after us.

—Bill Vaughn, *Kansas City Star*

Be good and you will be lonesome.

—Mark Twain

The difference between a moral man and a man of honor is that the latter regrets a discreditable act, even when it has worked and he has not been caught.

—H. L. Mencken

And from the eighteenth century:

Is there no hope? the sick man said;
The silent doctor shook his head.
And took his leave with signs of sorrow.
Despairing of his fee tomorrow.
—John Gay, "The Sick Man and the Angel"

Another face of cynicism is the pleasant recognition of man's foibles. Here you take a whimsical approach to human frailty.

The pride of ancestry increases in the ratio of distance.

—George W. Curtis

A boy is a man with some dirt on him.

No one is thirstier than the child reluctantly gone to bed.

There's only one pretty child in the world, and every mother has it.

—English proverb

A lot of people never get interested in a thing until they are told it is none of their business.

When a mother was disciplining her small boy, he begged, "Don't say 'must' mother. It makes me feel 'won't' all over."

—Eleanor L. Doan

ICONOCLASM

Because there is a basic urge in all of us—to a lesser or greater degree—to bring down the mighty, to break idols, a final way to endear yourself to your audience is to pose as an iconoclast. In iconoclasm wit has a holiday.

Perched on the loftiest throne in the world, man is still sitting on his own behind.

—Montaigne

For there was never yet philosopher
That could endure the toothache patiently.

—William Shakespeare

It is an interesting question how men would retain their relative rank if they were divested of their clothes.

—Henry David Thoreau

Hell, by the time a man scratches his ass, clears his throat, and tells me how smart he is, we've already wasted fifteen minutes.

—Lyndon B. Johnson

INDEX

DATE DUE

DEMCO 38-297